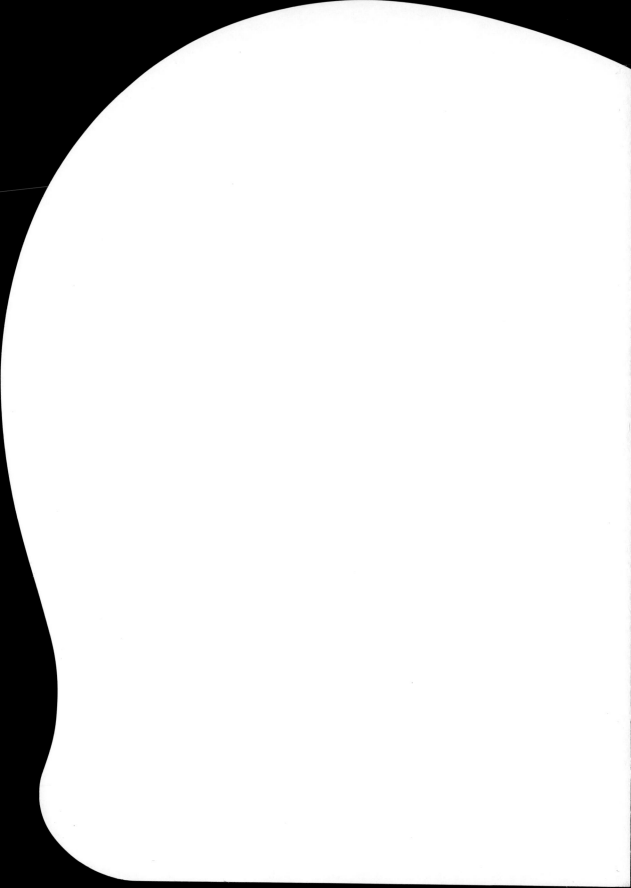

Crochet Hats!

Crochet Hats!

15 Stylish Projects to Top It All Off

CANDI JENSEN

Storey Publishing

The mission of Storey Publishing is to serve our customers by publishing practical information that encourages personal independence in harmony with the environment.

Edited by Gwen Steege
Art direction by Cynthia McFarland
Cover and text design by Cynthia McFarland
Text production by Jennifer Jepson Smith
Cover and interior photographs by Kevin Kennefick
Project styling by Wendy Scofield
Illustrations by Brigita Fuhrmann
Technical editing by Dee Neer
Indexed by Susan Olason, Indexes & Knowledge Maps

Printed in Hong Kong by Elegance
10 9 8 7 6 5 4 3 2 1

Library of Congress Cataloging-in-Publication Data
Jensen, Candi.
    Crochet hats! : 15 stylish projects to top it all off / Candi Jensen.
        p. cm.
    Includes index.
    ISBN-13: 978-1-58017-632-3; ISBN-10: 1-58017-632-1 (die-cut paper over board : alk. paper)
1. Crocheting—Patterns. 2. Hats. I. Title.

TT825.J4657 2006
746.43'40432—dc22

                                                                    2006015033

CONTENTS

Hats Off to Crocheting! 6

Warming Up 17

Straw Sun Hat 32

Ribbon Yarn Cap 38

Sherbet-Topped Baby 42

Tahoe Ski Hat 46

Pearl-Beaded Cap 52

Faux-Suede Helmet 56

Colorful Sun Hat 62

Fair Isle Hat 68

Angora & Diamonds 72

Retro Flowers 76

Gold-Chain Juliet 82

Dressy Cloche 86

Flower Child 90

Aran-Style Cables 96

Tweed & Bobbles 102

Acknowledgments 108

Sources 109

Index 110

Hats Off
to Crocheting!

With the busy schedules we all keep, it's hard to imagine stuffing one more thing onto our plates, but taking time for creativity can be a relaxing complement to everything else that's going on in a hectic life. And crocheting a hat is fast and fun!

A hat is much more than just something to protect your head from the cold: It can be a fashion statement, a real sign of your personality. Hat projects are small enough to carry with you wherever you go, and you don't have to worry about losing your place if you put them down and pick them up again later. Since they're so small, they're also perfect when you want to tackle a new stitch or try something beyond what you think you're capable of.

This book is chockfull of designs for every age and every skill level, from "so simple" to "I'm so impressed." You'll find an adorable baby cap (an ideal shower gift), a cute-as-can-be sun hat for a little princess, a sparkly little number to wear to a party, and a few hats for pulling on when you're playing outside. Many will work for both genders as well, with just a little tweaking of the colors. Hats for every season and occasion include sun hats, cabled hats, hats with brims, and hats with beads — even a couple of earflap hats to keep you cozy and warm.

As you work your way through this book, I hope you'll feel free to experiment with a pattern that you might feel is challenging or a little above your skill level. A hat is a really great way to gain those skills. Even if you have to pull out stitches, you don't have to rip so much. When I was first learning to crochet, I remember proudly bringing my almost-complete project to my teacher, then her telling me there was a mistake in the second row — as she wildly ripped out all my stitches. At that point, I realized that from then on I would learn new stitches or tackle challenging patterns on something small — fewer rows to rip out. I also resolved to pay more attention and became very proficient in crochet to lessen the chances of having future projects ripped out.

As you try out the various hats, I hope you're inspired to experiment with different color combinations or different types of yarn from those I used. Exploring new ideas is a fun way to make each hat your own. Most of all, I hope you will enjoy this book and spend many happy hours working on hats for yourself and all your loved ones.

Hooking Up

Although there are several different types of crochet hooks, they all have one thing in common: a hook at the end. Most hooks are made of aluminum, plastic, or wood; hooks for use with very fine yarns are often made of steel.

You catch and manipulate the yarn with the *head* and the *throat*, which are located at the end of the crochet hook. Behind the head is the *shank*, followed by a flat portion that is called the *grip*, and finally the *handle*. The flat portion is where you place your fingers to control the hook. Steel hooks sometimes have a thicker plastic handle that makes them easier to grip.

DIAGRAM OF A HOOK

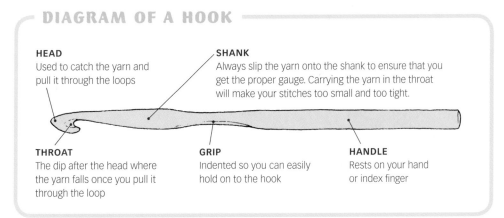

HEAD
Used to catch the yarn and pull it through the loops

SHANK
Always slip the yarn onto the shank to ensure that you get the proper gauge. Carrying the yarn in the throat will make your stitches too small and too tight.

THROAT
The dip after the head where the yarn falls once you pull it through the loop

GRIP
Indented so you can easily hold on to the hook

HANDLE
Rests on your hand or index finger

Yummy Yarns

From novelty yarns to sleek and smooth ones, the options are endless. We are lucky enough to live in a time when the yarn world provides us with a vast cornucopia of choice. I love to use as many different types as possible!

Putting a thought into yarn choices before you begin can save a few problems later on. If you can crochet with it, you can use it, although some fibers are certainly more appropriate for specific shapes and styles. You wouldn't want to use a very slinky, soft yarn for a hat that needs a stiff brim. On the other hand, if your hat pattern is lacy and open, you wouldn't choose a thick, woolly yarn. Or if you're working an intricate pattern stitch, you wouldn't want to completely hide the pattern with a novelty yarn that's furry, hairy or feathery.

Wearability is another factor to consider when you're looking around for the perfect yarn. If you're making a hat for the winter cold, you probably don't want it to be crocheted in a cotton. Conversely, if it's a sun hat, a wool might not be appropriate, as it would probably cause you to be too warm. Considering your choice of fiber is important to the type of project, but it needn't limit your creativity. Just use your common sense and you'll be fine.

Even though these projects are fairly small, it's worth determining how much yarn you need to complete your project, then buying enough of it up front. Yarn dye lots can vary quite a bit. If you go back for another skein later, you may end up with a sudden color shift that wasn't planned. It's also frustrating to be almost finished with the perfect hat for that special gift and run out of yarn. Most yarn stores will take back unused balls for credit — which gives you the perfect excuse to buy more yarn for your next project!

At the beginning of each project, I have given you a "generic" suggestion for the fiber content and yarn weight that I think is appropriate, and I've also given you information about the specific yarn I used for the hats that were photographed for the book. If you'd like to use the same yarn I did for a hat, keep in mind that manufacturers sometimes discontinue particular yarns or colors. Some of the yarns illustrated may not be available anymore. I do my best to choose yarns that will be available when the book is in your hands, but ultimately that is beyond my control. If you can't obtain the yarn listed for a project, contact the manufacturer and ask for a replacement yarn recommendation or use my advice as to a generic choice.

WEIGHT AND PLY

Once you start learning about yarns, you'll want to know about their weight, which is usually identified on the yarn label as one of six gradations: super fine (sock, fingering, baby), fine (sport, baby), light (DK, light worsted), medium (worsted, afghan, aran), bulky (chunky, craft, rug), and super bulky (bulky, roving). The ply, or number of strands of yarn that have been twisted together to form your yarn, is also often listed and usually runs from single- to 4-ply.

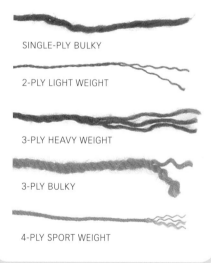

SINGLE-PLY BULKY

2-PLY LIGHT WEIGHT

3-PLY HEAVY WEIGHT

3-PLY BULKY

4-PLY SPORT WEIGHT

Language of Crochet

Probably the most difficult thing about learning to crochet isn't the technique: It's the shorthand used in many patterns. At first glance, it looks as if the designer has an aversion to vowels, but in fact, directions are filled with abbreviations in order to make a pattern seem shorter. Don't let this intimidate you. Although I've minimized the use of abbreviations in this book, it's worthwhile to learn the abbreviations right from the beginning, since you'll find them in most patterns. Refer to the list on page 11 whenever you feel brain fatigue and can't remember what "sc" means. You may want make a copy of this list and keep it with whatever pattern you're working on.

TERMS

Some of the crochet terms that you will run into are not abbreviated, but they still are a kind of shorthand that means something very specific to crocheters.

Pattern. The instructions for any given project

Front loop. The loop closest to you at the top of the stitch

Back loop. The loop on the other side of the stitch

Post. The vertical area of the stitch

Right side. The side of your piece that will show

Wrong side. The back side of your piece

Right-hand side. The side on the right as you are looking at it while crocheting

Left-hand side. The side on the left as you are looking at it while crocheting

Work even. Following the pattern as it has been established

Yarn over. Wrapping the yarn around the hook from back to front

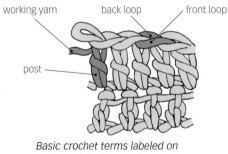

Basic crochet terms labeled on a piece of double crochet

SYMBOLS

, ∗, †. Asterisks, stars, and daggers are used to mark the beginning of a sequence of steps that you will need to repeat across a row or in a round. In the following example, you would follow the steps from the "" to the semi-colon twice:

Example

* Single crochet in the next 2 stitches, skip 1 stitch, single crochet in the next 2 stitches; repeat from * one more time.

(), []. Parentheses or brackets are often used to enclose a set of steps within another set of steps. In the next example, the steps within the parentheses are all worked in one of the chain stitches. The entire sequence is worked three times.

Example

* 3 double crochet in next chain-1 space, chain 1, (3 double crochet, chain 2, 3 double crochet) in next chain-2 space, chain 1; repeat from * two more times.

ABBREVIATIONS

alt	alternate		**patt**	pattern
beg	begin, beginning		**prev**	previous
bl(s)	back loop(s)		**rem**	remain, remaining
CA	contrasting color A		**rep**	repeat, repeating
CB	contrasting color B		**rnd(s)**	round(s)
CC	contrasting color C or contrasting color		**sc**	single crochet
			sc2tog	single crochet two together
ch(s)	chain(s)		**sk**	skip
dc	double crochet		**sl**	slip
dc2tog	double crochet two together		**sl st**	slip stitch
dec	decrease, decreasing		**sp**	space
fig	figure		**st(s)**	stitch(es)
fl(s)	front loop(s)		**tch**	turning chain
hdc	half double crochet		**tog**	together
hdc2tog	half double crochet two together		**tr**	triple, or treble, crochet
			yo	yarn over
inc	increase			

Be Sage, Check Your Gauge

Gauge is the number of stitches and rows in a given number of square inches, and it determines the finished measurement of your work. Before you start any project, it's really important to check your gauge! This should become your mantra whenever you start a crochet project. You want that hat to snuggle right down over your head, not perch up on top of it or fall down over your eyes!

Because most patterns tell you what size hook and yarn to use, it's tempting to just skip over the gauge and expect things to come out fine. However, hook sizes are not standard. What one company calls a size F might be a size G somewhere else. Also, you may have a different way of holding the hook or tightening the yarn that can dramatically affect the finished size of your work.

It's more important to match the number of stitches and rows listed in the gauge than it is to use the designated hook size. This is why the hook requirements in pattern directions are usually followed by the note *"or size you need to obtain correct gauge."*

MAKING A GAUGE SWATCH

To check your gauge for any given pattern, crochet a swatch using the hook size and yarn indicated. Lay a ruler horizontally over the finished swatch and count the number of stitches within the required number of inches. If you have too many stitches, your stitches need to be bigger, so try again with a larger hook. If you don't have enough stitches, your stitches need to be smaller, so try a smaller hook.

Turn your ruler sideways to count the number of rows. You may not get both the stitches and the rows exactly right. Aim for the correct number of stitches, as you can usually crochet more or fewer rows to adjust the length of a project.

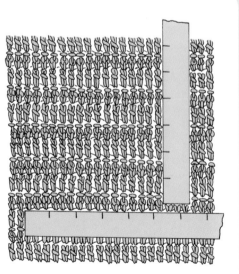

Beads, Beautiful Beads

Adding a little sparkle or interest to your crochet hat is easy when you think of beads. They can transform a simple everyday cap into a glowing masterpiece, as in the Pearl-Beaded Cap (page 52). Try adding a few beads to the ends of ties or braids, or crochet a few beads into an edging. You can also incorporate beads into bobbles at the center of flowers to make them more your own work of art or add them to flower petals — they'll look like shimmering dewdrops!

Before you begin, thread the number of beads you need onto your yarn. Push them down out of the way while you make the chain and ring, then bring one in each time you draw up a loop. To ensure that the beads are positioned on the *right* side, the *wrong* side of the piece should be facing you when you work in the beads.

The beads in the Pearl-Beaded Cap are worked in single crochet in the round. Instead of continuing around, however, you must turn at the end of each row so that you can work the beads on wrong-side rows as follows: At the beginning of the row,

Working a bead into a crocheted piece

THREADING TRICKS

■ Depending on the weight of the yarn and the size of the beads, it may be difficult to thread them onto the yarn. To overcome this problem, thread a regular sewing needle with a 10-inch length of thread, line up the thread ends, and knot them together. Draw the end of the yarn through the two threads, leaving about 6 inches of the yarn hanging down. Thread a bead onto the needle, draw it down the thread and then down onto the yarn.

■ The tip of the yarn may become dirty or frayed during the bead stringing. Be sure to clip off the damaged part before you begin to crochet.

ch 1, * sc in next stitch, pull up a bead, ch 1, skip 1; repeat from * to end of row, join with a slip stitch to first stitch, turn. The beads in the Straw Sun Hat (page 32) are worked similarly in double crochet.

BEADED EDGINGS

Any crocheted piece can be transformed if you work beads along an edge. Depending on the style of the beads, your project will suddenly become more fun, more elegant, or more off-beat! Here's one way to proceed:

String beads on your yarn until you have the number you need. (To determine this, measure the edging, figure out how closely you want to space the beads, then divide the spacing into the total measurement. You may want to add a few extra beads to be sure you don't run out.)

Set Up Join yarn to the lower right edge. With wrong side of the piece facing you, work * 1 single crochet in first stitch, chain 1, skip 1; repeat from * across edge, chain 2, turn.

Row 1 (right side) * Slide up bead against work, chain 2, 1 single crochet in chain-1 space; repeat from * across edge. End with 1 single crochet in chain-1 space. Chain 4, turn.

Row 2 * 1 single crochet in single crochet, chain 3; repeat from * across. End 1 single crochet in last single crochet. Chain 2, turn.

Row 3 * Slide bead against work, chain 2, 1 single crochet into chain-3 space, chain 1; repeat from * across. End 1 single crochet in second chain of chain-4. Draw yarn through last stitch to fasten off, and then break yarn.

Finishes and Flourishes

You can always leave the crown of your hat plain, but if you want to add a flourish, here are two favorites: pompoms and tassels.

POMPOMS

These fuzzy balls can be as large or as small as you like. The following directions are for a standard size.

❶ Cut a block of cardboard that is half as wide as you want your pompom to be.

❷ Wrap yarn around the cardboard 50–125 times, depending on the pompom's diameter and the yarn's weight. Smaller pompoms need fewer wraps than larger pompoms; pompoms made with heavy yarn need fewer wraps as well. Keep the strands evenly spaced and don't overlap them too much in the center.

❸ Insert an 8" (20 cm) length of yarn under the bundle of yarn at the top of the cardboard. Draw the ends of the short piece around the bundle and knot them securely together.

❹ Slip the tip of your scissors under the yarn at the opposite edge of the cardboard and cut through all layers.

❺ Remove the cardboard, and trim the yarn ends to neaten. (Do not cut the yarn you used to tie the bundle together.)

❻ Use the ends of the yarn tie to attach the pompom to the hat by threading them one by one through a large-eye yarn needle and drawing each end to the inside of the hat. Tie the ends in a square knot and weave in the loose ends.

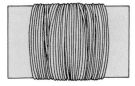

Step 2

Steps 3 & 4

TASSELS

The method for making tassels is similar to that for pompoms. Tassels can be as short or as long as you like.

❶ Cut a block of cardboard that is the length you want your tassel to be.

❷ Wrap yarn around the cardboard 25 times for medium weight yarns and 15 times for bulky weights.

❸ Insert an 8" (20 cm) length of yarn under the bundle of yarn at the top of the cardboard. Draw the ends of the short piece around the bundle and knot them securely together.

❹ Slip the tip of your scissors under the yarn at the opposite edge of the cardboard and cut through all layers. Remove the cardboard.

❺ Wrap another 8" (20 cm) length of yarn around the tassel ¾" (2 cm) below the previous knot, tie it tightly, and let the ends blend into the rest of the tassel.

❻ Cut the loose ends to the same length. (Do not cut the yarn you used to tie the bundle together at the top.)

❼ Use the ends of the yarn tie to attach the tassel to the hat by threading them one by one through a large-eye yarn needle and drawing each end to the inside of the hat. Tie the ends in a square knot and weave in the loose ends.

Making a tassel

Steps 3 & 4   *Step 5*

IN YOUR CROCHET BAG

I'm assuming you're going to love crochet so much you'll start doing it everywhere, in which case you'll need what we experts refer to as a crochet bag. Here are some things you'll want to stash there:

- Crochet hooks, sizes F through I
- Yarn
- Safety pins
- Large-eye yarn needle
- Sharp sewing scissors
- Tape measure and ruler
- List of abbreviations and a photocopy of your pattern
- Nail file
- Notebook and pen or pencil
- Calculator
- Sticky tags to mark your place in the pattern
- Open-sided stitch markers

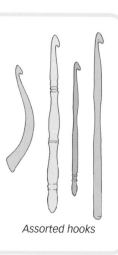

Assorted hooks

Warming Up

Finally, we get to the fun part — let's pick up that hook and yarn and actually begin to crochet. Experienced crocheters can skip right to the patterns. If you're new to crochet, try out these basic stitches and you'll be tackling the projects before you know it!

My babysitter taught me to crochet when I was seven years old because she thought it would keep me quiet. Little did she know what she was starting. I never felt comfortable with the way she held her yarn, so I developed my own way. I encourage you to experiment and find what feels right to you. Once you've learned how to do a single crochet (sc), double crochet (dc), half double crochet (hdc), and triple crochet (tr), you can crochet almost any project. It's surprising how much you can accomplish with a few simple loops!

HANDS ON!

For practice, use a medium hook, like a G or an H, which is easy to maneuver. Select a smooth, worsted-weight yarn, such as 100% wool, so the hook will slide in and out of the loops easily and you can see the structure of the stitches. It also helps to see what you're doing if you work with light-colored yarn. After just a bit of practice, you'll be amazed at how quickly you catch on.

Holding the Hook

Pick up your crochet hook and hold it pretty much the way you hold a pen or a fork. You need to hold on to it tightly enough to control it easily, but keep your fingers relaxed. You don't have to choke the life out of the thing!

Two options for holding the hook

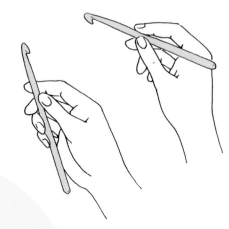

HOOK CONVERSION

In the United States, hooks are sized in either letters (B through S) or numbers (1 through 16). In the metric and English equivalents, only numbers are used. The patterns in this book give both the U.S. sizes and the metric equivalents.

Approximate Hook Sizes

U.S. (American)	Continental (metric)	U.K. (English)
B/1	2.5 mm	12
C/2	3 mm	11
D/3	3.25 mm	10
E/4	3.5 mm	9
F/5	4 mm	8
G/6	4.25 mm	7
7	4.5 mm	7
H/8	5 mm	6
I/9	5.5 mm	5
J/10	6 mm	4
K/10.5	7 mm	3
L/11	8 mm	–
M/13	9 mm	–
N/15	10 mm	–
P/16	15 mm	–
Q	16 mm	–
S	19 mm	–

Holding the Yarn

There are many ways to hold the yarn, and once again it comes down to what feels right to you. I've given the two most common versions below.

Option 1: Loop the yarn over the index finger of your left hand. Hold the working end (the end coming from the skein or ball) loosely with the last two fingers of that hand. You can use these fingers to adjust the tension on the yarn as you draw the yarn along. Use your thumb and middle finger to hold the loop and the tail of the yarn.

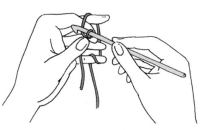

Option 2: Wrap the yarn around the little finger of your left hand, and then drape it over your middle finger. Use your thumb and index finger to hold the loop and the tail of the yarn.

SLIP KNOT

Crochet begins with a single loop and then builds from there. Now that you have the hook and the yarn worked out, it's time to make that first loop.

1 Leaving a tail of about 6" (15 cm), make a loop.

2 With your crochet hook, reach through the loop and catch the tail end with the hook.

3 Pull the yarn toward you through the loop.

4 Tighten the knot on the hook.

CHAIN (CH)

Once you have a slip knot on your hook, you can start to crochet. Everything starts with the beginning chain.

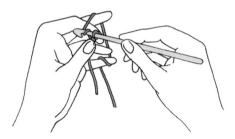

1 Bring the yarn over the hook from back to front, catch it with the hook, and then pull it through the slip knot. Slip the loop you've just made to the shank of the hook, or the stitch will be too small.

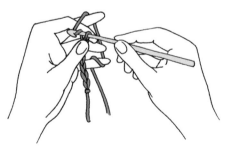

2 Repeat the process. Try to get a nice even tension. If you pull too hard, the chain will be too tight. If you don't give it enough tension, it will be too loose.

Working with the Chain

Let's take a look at the structure of the chain. Notice that the front of the chain looks like a series of interlocking Vs.

The back of the chain looks like a series of bumps.

To count the number of chains, never count either the slip knot or the loop on the hook. To achieve the correct number, it helps to count out the chains as you pull the loops through each time.

There are 6 chains in the above illustration.

SINGLE CROCHET (SC)

Now that you're comfortable with the whole chain concept, you can start to learn the stitches. All crochet projects begin with a chain, so chain 6 (ch 6) to practice the single crochet. If you make a mistake, just pull out the stitches and start over. You aren't making anything yet — this is practice, and there are no crochet police watching over your shoulder.

Row 1

❶ To begin the first row of single crochet, make 6 chain stitches, then insert the hook through the second chain from the hook.

❷ Bring the yarn over the hook from the back to the front.

❸ Pull the yarn to the front and move it to the shank of the hook. There are now two loops on the hook.

④ Bring the yarn over the hook again from back to front and pull it through both loops on the hook.

⑤ Now you have one loop on the hook, and you have completed 1 single crochet.

⑥ Insert the hook into the next chain and repeat the process until you have reached the end of the chain. Do not crochet into the slip knot itself. You should see five stitches in the completed row. Don't forget to count as you work.

TIP

Remember, as you work your first row of single crochet, it's important not to twist the chain: Always keep the front facing you.

Row 2

⑦ Before you turn to work a second row of single crochet, chain 1. This is called the *turning chain*. Now, turn the piece counter-clockwise so the back is facing you.

⑧ Work the first single crochet into the last single crochet of the previous row. This time, insert the hook under both top loops of the first single crochet and repeat steps 2–5.

⑨ Continue in this way across the row and subsequent rows until the piece is the desired length. You'll find it helps to count stitches as you work, so that you don't gain or lose any. There should be five single crochet when you complete this row.

⑩ To end, cut the yarn, leaving about a 6" (15 cm) tail, then pull the yarn completely through the last loop to fasten off.

DOUBLE CROCHET (DC)

Double crochet is similar to single crochet, only with a few more steps. Double crochet is a taller stitch, so you need to start with a chain that is a little longer. To practice, start with a chain of 11 stitches.

Row 1

1 Bring the yarn over the hook from the back to the front. Insert the hook into the fourth chain from the hook.

2 Bring the yarn over the hook again (from the back), pull it through to the front, and move it to the shank. You now have three loops on the hook.

3 Bring the yarn over the hook a third time and draw it through the first two loops on the hook.

4 You now have two loops on the hook.

5 Bring the yarn over again from back to front and pull it through the two remaining loops on the hook.

6 You have now completed a double crochet.

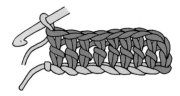

7 Repeat steps 1–6 across the row, working in the next chain for each stitch.

Row 2

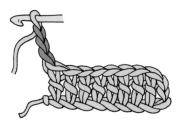

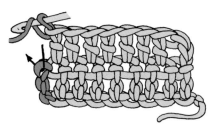

8 Before turning your work to start a second row, crochet 3 chain stitches. This *turning chain* is the start of the second row, and you need to make one at the end of each row of double crochet.

10 Insert the hook into the top chain of the turning chain and complete your last double crochet.

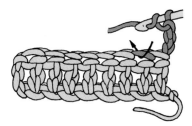

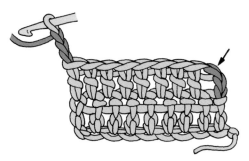

9 Turn the work counterclockwise. Yarn over from back to front, insert the hook into the top two loops of the second chain from the hook, then repeat steps 2–6. Continue in this way, inserting the hook into the top two loops of each stitch to the end of the row.

11 Make a chain-3 turning chain as before. Turn, and crochet to the end of the next row, then work the last double crochet in the top stitch of the turning chain from the previous row (at arrow). There are 8 double crochet (not counting the turning chain) in each completed row.

HALF DOUBLE CROCHET (HDC)

As the name implies, the half double crochet takes one step out of the double crochet, thereby making it a shorter stitch. It is also a little thicker because you work through three loops at the same time. Once again, start with a chain of 11.

Row 1

❶ Bring the yarn over the hook from the back to the front. Insert the hook into the third chain from the hook.

❷ Yarn over and draw the yarn through the chain to the front, then move it to the shank of the hook. You now have three loops on the hook.

❸ Yarn over again from back to front and pull it through all three loops on the hook.

❹ You have now completed a half double crochet.

❺ Repeat these steps in each chain across the row.

Row 2

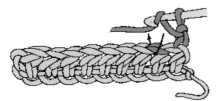

6 Before turning your work to start a second row, crochet 2 chain stitches. This *turning chain* is the start of the second row, and you need to make one at the end of each row of half double crochet. Yarn over and insert the hook into the second stitch in the row.

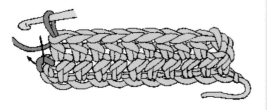

7 Repeat the steps for half double crochet across the row, working into both top loops of each stitch until you get to the chain 2 (turning chain) of the previous row. There are 9 half double crochet, not counting the turning chain, in each completed row.

8 Insert the hook into the top chain of the turning chain and complete your last half double crochet. Make a chain-2 turning chain and turn as before.

TRIPLE CROCHET (TR)

The triple crochet is taller and has one step more than the double crochet. Begin by chaining 11.

Row 1

1 Bring the yarn over the hook twice from the back to the front.

2 Insert the hook into the fifth chain from the hook and yarn over.

3 Pull the yarn through the chain to the front and move it to the shank of the hook. You now have four loops on the hook.

4 Bring the yarn over again from back to front and pull it through the first two loops on the hook. You now have three loops on the hook.

5 Yarn over again. Pull the yarn through the next two loops on the hook.

6 You now have two loops on the hook.

7 Yarn over one more time and pull the yarn through the last two loops on the hook to complete the stitch.

8 Repeat these steps across the row.

Row 2

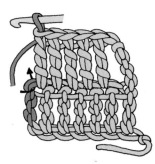

9 Before turning your work to start a second row, crochet 4 chain stitches. This *turning chain* is the start of the second row, and you need to make one at the end of each row of triple crochet.

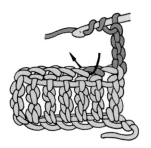

10 Turn the work counterclockwise. Yarn over twice and insert the hook under both top loops of the second stitch from the hook. Repeat steps 3–7.

11 Continue in this way, working into both top loops of each stitch across the row, until you get to the chain 4 (turning chain) of the previous row. Insert the hook into the top chain of the turning chain and complete your last triple crochet. There are 6 triple crochet, not counting the turning chain, in each completed row.

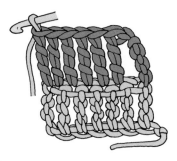

12 Make a chain-4 turning chain and turn as before.

SLIP STITCH (SL ST)

The slip stitch is a way of joining or moving across a stitch without adding height or another stitch. The first four stitches at the right of the drawing are slip stitches, allowing you to move to the fifth stitch up without adding height.

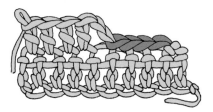

Here's how to do one slip stitch: Insert the hook into the top loops of the stitch and draw yarn through those loops and the loop on the hook without any yarn overs.

WORKING WITH CIRCLES

The basis for a huge family of crochet projects is a circle, created by making a chain and then joining the ends of the chain with a slip stitch. Many of the hats in this book begin just this way. Mastering the circle opens the door to all kinds of projects, including not only the hats themselves, but also decorative elements like flowers. Once you've made the initial circle (referred to as a *ring*), you can work any stitch — single crochet, double crochet, and so on — into that circle.

To join stitches into a circle, chain 4, then insert your hook into the first chain. Yarn over, and then draw the yarn through both the chain and the loop on the hook with no further yarn overs (slip stitch).

NO KNOTS

You should never knot two ends of yarn together when crocheting. Not only does this create an unsightly bump or hole in the finished piece, but it almost always eventually pops through to the right side of the fabric — and reveals your shortcut!

28

To work double crochet in a 4-chain ring, chain 3. Like a turning chain, this chain is needed in order to get you up to the height of the double crochet stitches, even though you don't turn when working in circles. Work the double crochet by inserting your hook into the ring (not into the chains) and proceeding as described on page 22.

To join the circle, insert the hook into the top chain of the beginning chain 3. Yarn over, then draw the yarn through the top chain and the loop on the hook with no further yarn overs (slip stitch).

JOINING A NEW BALL OF YARN

At some point in most projects, you will use up one ball of yarn and need to add another. Not to worry; joining yarn is easy. The best plan is to make the switch at the end of a row or round, so you don't have stray strands of yarn in the middle of your work. When you see the tail end of your yarn coming up, make the join at the beginning of the next row. Here's how it's done:

Work until you have two loops left on the hook. Draw the new yarn through the two loops to finish the stitch using the new yarn. Leave 6" (15 cm) tails on both old and new yarns so that you can weave them into the wrong side later.

Guess what? This same technique works for changing colors. Unless your pattern says otherwise, always switch to a new color at the end of a row or round.

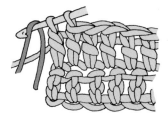

FINISHING

Once you complete a project, you need to know how to finish it properly. Most of the hats in this book are crocheted in a circle and shaped in such a way that you need do little more than weave any yarn tails into the wrong side and you're done. For a few, however, you'll need to sew a short seam. Each of the patterns in the book has specific finishing instructions if required. Here is some general advice on how to give your hat its well-deserved final touches.

Weaving in Ends

Take up one of your loose ends and thread it through a large-eye yarn needle. Working on the wrong side of the piece, weave the yarn in and out along a row for about 2" (5 cm). Now turn your work counterclockwise and, still working on the wrong side, weave it in the other direction for a few more stitches, to lock it in place. Snip off any excess yarn close to the piece.

Although it may be tempting to save time and effort by weaving more than one end in at a time, resist temptation! Doubled yarns create a telltale lump that is sure to show. Also, make certain that your weaving isn't visible on the right side of the work. If you weave in the ends well, they shouldn't show on either the right or wrong side.

Sewing Pieces Together

You'll run into two basic situations when it comes to joining crocheted pieces: seaming side edges together and seaming top or bottom edges together. In this book, the hats that need a seam are joined along side edges, which means you work with row stitches. Here's how to do it:

Carefully match the edges so that the rows align. Using matching yarn, thread a large-eye yarn needle, and then weave the yarn in and out of corresponding loops on each edge, as in the illustration. This technique is known as *mattress stitch*.

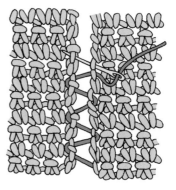

Straw Sun Hat

Have fun in the sun with this "Beadalicious" straw hat. Worked in a novel raffia yarn with shell-stitched edge and chunky beads, it puts the perfect new spin on a favorite basic look. Try this hat in a number of different color combinations and beads.

Finished measurement
22" (55.9 cm) circumference

Yarn
Raffia-type yarn, 2 skeins of natural
I used Judi and Co. Raffia, 100% rayon,
72 yds (65.8 m)
Natural, 2 balls

Hook
US H/8 (5 mm), *or size you need to obtain correct gauge*

Gauge
12 sts and 9 rows = 4" × 4" (10 cm × 10 cm) in hdc

Other supplies
Large-eye yarn needle
22 assorted beads, ¼–½" (6–12 mm)

Abbreviations
ch = chain
dc = double crochet
hdc = half double crochet
sc = single crochet

CROCHETING THE HAT

NOTE	At the end of each round, join with a slip stitch to first stitch, but do not turn unless otherwise indicated. (Two of the rows in the beaded band are worked back and forth, with turns at the end of each row.)
SET UP	Ch 4, join with a slip stitch in first chain to form a ring.
Round 1	Ch 1, 8 sc into ring, join with a slip stitch to first sc. *You now have* 8 sc.
Round 2	Ch 1, 2 hdc in each sc, join with a slip stitch to first hdc. *You now have* 16 hdc.
Round 3	Ch 1, * 2 hdc in first hdc, 1 hdc in next stitch; repeat from * around, join with a slip stitch to first hdc. *You now have* 24 hdc.
Round 4	Ch 1, * 1 hdc in next 2 stitches, 2 hdc in next stitch; repeat from * around, join with a slip stitch to first hdc. *You now have* 32 hdc.
Round 5	Ch 1, * 1 hdc in next 3 stitches, 2 hdc in next stitch; repeat from * around, join with a slip stitch to first hdc. *You now have* 40 hdc.
Round 6	Ch 1, * 1 hdc in next 4 stitches, 2 hdc in next stitch; repeat from * around, join with a slip stitch to first hdc. *You now have* 48 hdc.
Round 7	Ch 1, * 1 hdc in next 5 stitches, 2 hdc in next stitch; repeat from * around, join with a slip stitch to first hdc. *You now have* 56 hdc.
Round 8	Ch 1, * 1 hdc in next 6 stitches, 2 hdc in next stitch; repeat from * around, join with a slip stitch to first hdc. *You now have* 64 hdc.
Rounds 9 and 10	Ch 1, 1 hdc in each stitch around, join with a slip stitch to first hdc.
Round 11	Ch 1, * 1 hdc in next 31 stitches, 2 hdc in next stitch; repeat from * one more time, join with a slip stitch to first hdc. *You now have* 66 hdc.
Round 12	Ch 1, 1 hdc in each stitch around, join with a slip stitch to first hdc.

	Draw yarn through last stitch to fasten off, then cut yarn. Weave loose ends into back of hat.
CROCHETING THE BEADED BAND	
SET UP	String 22 beads onto the yarn.
NOTE	Rounds 1 and 3 in this section are worked with the wrong side of the hat facing you. This ensures that the beads are positioned on the right side of the hat. Note that you must turn at the beginning and end of each of these two rows in order to work on the wrong side. Rounds 2 and 4 and all other rounds are worked as for the crown, joining at the end of each round with a slip stitch, with no turn. (See also page 13.)
Round 1 (wrong side)	Join yarn at the place where you stopped, ch 3, turn (wrong side is now facing you). * Skip 2 stitches, (2 dc, pull up bead, ch 1 loosely, 2 dc) in next stitch, skip 2 stitches, dc in next stitch; repeat from * to end of round, join with a slip stitch to top of ch-3, ch 1, turn.
Round 2	1 hdc in each stitch, including the ch-1 behind the bead, to end of round, join with a slip stitch to the first hdc, ch 3, turn.
Round 3 (wrong side)	* (2 dc, pull up bead, ch 1 loosely, 2 dc) in next stitch, skip 2 stitches, dc in next stitch; repeat from * to end of round, join with a slip stitch to top of ch-3, turn.
Round 4	Ch 1, 1 hdc in each stitch, including the ch 1 behind the bead, to end of round, join with a slip stitch to the ch-1. (From Round 4 to end, do not turn at the ends of rounds.)
Rounds 5 and 6	Ch 1, 1 hdc in each stitch to end of round, join with a slip stitch to ch-1.
CROCHETING THE BRIM	
Round 1	Ch 1, working in front loop only, * 1 hdc in next 2 stitches, 2 hdc in next stitch; repeat from * to end of round, join with a slip stitch to the ch-1. *You now have 88 hdc.*

Round 2	Ch 1, hdc in both loops of each stitch to end of round, join with a slip stitch to the ch-1.
Round 3	Ch 1, * 1 hdc in next 3 stitches, 2 hdc in next stitch; repeat from * to end of round, join with a slip stitch to the ch-1. *You now have* 110 hdc.
Round 4	Ch 1, hdc in each stitch to end of round, join with a slip stitch to the ch-1.
Round 5	Ch 1, * hdc in next 4 stitches, 2 hdc in next stitch; repeat from * to end of round, join with a slip stitch to the ch-1. *You now have* 132 hdc.
Round 6	Ch 1, * 1 hdc in next stitch, skip 2 stitches, work 5 dc in next stitch, skip 2 stitches; repeat from * to end of round, join with a slip stitch to the ch-1.
FINISHING	
	Draw yarn through last stitch to fasten off, then cut yarn. Weave loose ends into back of hat.

OTHER YARNS TO TRY

Judi and Co. Raffia, 100% viscose raffia, 100 yds (91 m): (from top to bottom) Plum, Jade Orchid, Brown

Ribbon Yarn Cap

Dress up a drab day with a bright ribbon cap. Perfect for daytime or evening, it's worked in a basic single crochet with dainty shell stitches across the middle to add a little decorative touch. The ribbon yarn is easy to work with and has just a hint of shine.

Finished measurement
21" (53.3 cm) circumference

Yarn
Medium-weight ribbon yarn, two balls of light green
I used Berroco Zen, 40% cotton/60% nylon, 1¾ oz (50 g)/110 yds (102 m)
Wasabi #8229, 2 balls

Hook
US H/8 (5 mm), *or size you need to obtain correct gauge*

Gauge
14 sts and 16 rows = 4" × 4" (10 cm × 10 cm) in sc

Other supplies
Large-eye yarn needle
Sewing thread to match ribbon yarn

Abbreviations
ch = chain
dc = double crochet
hdc = half double crochet
sc = single crochet

CROCHETING THE HAT	
Set Up	Ch 4, join with a slip stitch to form a ring.
Note	From here on, join with a slip stitch at the end of each round, but do not turn.
Round 1	Ch 1, work 8 sc into ring, join with a slip stitch to first sc.
Round 2	Ch 1, work 2 sc in each sc, join with a slip stitch to first stitch. *You now have* 16 sc.
Round 3	Ch 1, * sc in first sc, 2 sc in next sc; repeat from * around, join with a slip stitch to first stitch. *You now have* 24 sc.
Round 4	Ch 1, * sc in next 2 stitches, 2 sc in next stitch; repeat from * around, join with a slip stitch to first stitch. *You now have* 32 sc.
Round 5	Ch 1, * sc in next 3 stitches, 2 sc in next stitch; repeat from * around, join with a slip stitch to first stitch. *You now have* 40 sc.
Round 6	Ch 1, * sc in next 4 stitches, 2 sc in next stitch; repeat from * around, join with a slip stitch to first stitch. *You now have* 48 sc.
Round 7	Ch 1, * sc in next 5 stitches, 2 sc in next stitch; repeat from * around, join with a slip stitch to first stitch. *You now have* 56 sc.
Round 8	Ch 1, * sc in next 6 stitches, 2 sc in next stitch; repeat from * around, join with a slip stitch to first stitch. *You now have* 64 sc.
Rounds 9–11	Ch 1, sc in each stitch around, join with a slip stitch to first stitch.
Round 12	Ch 1, * sc in next 7 stitches, 2 sc in next stitch; repeat from * around, join with a slip stitch to first stitch. *You now have* 72 sc.
Rounds 13–15	Ch 1, sc in each stitch around, join with a slip stitch to first stitch.

Round 16	Ch 2, * skip 2 stitches, 5 dc in next stitch, skip 2 stitches, hdc in next stitch; repeat from * around, ending with a slip stitch in top of ch-2 (instead of hdc), turn.
Rounds 17 and 19	Ch 1, * 5 dc in hdc, hdc in center dc of 5-dc of previous round; repeat from * around, ending with a slip stitch in first dc.
Rounds 18 and 20	Ch 1, * hdc in center of 5-dc, 5 dc in hdc; repeat from * around, ending with a slip stitch in first hdc.
Round 21	Ch 1, sc in each stitch around, join with a slip stitch to first stitch.
Next Rounds	Repeat Round 21 eight more times. Draw yarn through last stitch to fasten off, then break yarn. Weave loose ends into wrong side of hat.

TURNING THE HEM ON THE RIBBON HAT

Turn up the bottom edge (the last sc rounds) twice to form a cuff on the right side about 1" (2.5 cm) wide as shown. Use matching sewing thread to sew the cuff in place.

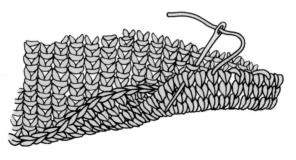

Sherbet-Topped Baby

Put a new spin on the tried-and-true ripple stitch with this fanciful baby hat. Self-striping yarn gives the hat a customized look without your having to change colors. Topped off with a great big pom pom for added fun.

Finished measurement
14" (35.5 cm) circumference

Yarn
Heavy worsted-weight yarn, 1 ball
I used Nashua Handknits Woolly Stripes, 100% wool, 1¾ oz (50 g)/88 yds (80 m) Color #4, 1 ball

Hook
US H/8 (5 mm), *or size you need to obtain correct gauge*

Gauge
16 sts and 12 rows = 4" × 4" (10 cm × 10 cm) in hdc

Other supplies
Large-eye yarn needle

Abbreviations
ch = chain
dc = double crochet
hdc = half double crochet
sc = single crochet

CROCHETING THE HAT	
NOTE	At the end of each round, join with a slip stitch to first stitch; do not turn.
SET UP	Ch 4, join with a slip stitch to first stitch to form a ring.
Round 1	Ch 1, 12 sc into ring, join with a slip stitch to first sc.
Round 2	Ch 1, 2 sc in each sc to end of round, join with a slip stitch to first stitch. *You now have* 24 sc.
Round 3	Ch 1, * sc in next 2 stitches, 2 sc in next stitch; repeat from * to end of round, join with a slip stitch to first stitch. *You now have* 32 sc.
Round 4	Sc in same sc as joining, * skip next sc, 3 dc in next sc, skip next sc, sc in next sc; repeat from * to end of round, skipping last sc, join with a slip stitch to first stitch. *You now have* eight 3-dc groups.
Round 5	Hdc in same stitch as joining, hdc in dc, * 3 hdc in next dc, hdc in each of next 3 stitches; repeat from * to last 2 stitches, 3 hdc in next dc, hdc in next dc, join with a slip stitch to first stitch. *You now have* 48 hdc.
Round 6	Hdc in first stitch, hdc in next stitch, * 3 hdc in next hdc (center of 3 hdc group), hdc in next 2 hdc, skip next hdc, hdc in next 2 hdc; repeat from * to last 2 hdc, hdc in these 2 stitches, join with a slip stitch to first stitch. *You now have* 56 hdc.
Round 7	Hdc in first stitch and in next hdc, * 3 hdc in next hdc, hdc in next 2 hdc, skip 2 hdc, hdc in next 2 hdc; repeat from * to last 3 stitches, 3 hdc in next hdc, hdc in next 2 hdc, join with a slip stitch to first stitch.
Rounds 8–15	Hdc in first stitch and in next hdc, * 3 hdc in next hdc, hdc in next 2 hdc, skip 2 hdc, hdc in next 2 hdc; repeat from * to last 3 stitches, 3 hdc in next hdc, hdc in next 2 hdc, join with a slip stitch to first stitch.

FINISHING

Draw yarn through last stitch to fasten off, then break yarn. Weave loose ends into wrong side of hat.

OTHER YARNS TO TRY

(from top to bottom)

Red Heart Soft, 100% acrylic, 5 oz (140 g)/256 yds (234 m): Turquoise #2515

Patons Kroy Socks (2 strands worked together), 75% wool/25% nylon, 1.75 oz. (50 g)/ 192 yds (174 m): Paint Box #54567

Wendy Velvet Touch, 100% nylon, 1.75 oz (50 g)/115 yds (105 m): PaleYellow #1206

Tahoe Ski Hat

Yo, Dude! Something for the guy in your life to keep warm while schussing down the slopes. The earflap cap makes a fashion statement these days, and this one is simply striped in a sumptuous alpaca. Such a great hat, you can make one for your hidden "dudette."

Finished measurement
22" (55.9 cm) circumference

Yarn
Light-weight worsted alpaca yarn: 1 ball each of natural, grey, medium blue, and dark grey
I used Classic Elite Inca Alpaca, 100% alpaca, 109 yds (100 m)/1¾ oz (50 g)
MC = Natural #1116, 1 skein
CA = Amarino Grey #1103, 1 skein
CB = Island of the Sun #1146, 1 skein
CC = Peruvian Earth #1109, 1 skein

Hook
US K/10.5 (6.5 or 7 mm), *or size you need to obtain correct gauge*

Gauge
9 sts and 8 rows = 4" × 4" (10 cm × 10 cm) in hdc

Other supplies
Large-eye yarn needle

Abbreviations
ch = chain
dc = double crochet
hdc = half double crochet
hdc2tog = half double crochet 2 together (see page 59)

CROCHETING THE HAT	
Set Up	Using MC doubled, ch 4, join with a slip stitch to first chain to form a ring, ch 1.
Note	In this section, join with a slip stitch to the first stitch at the end of each round, but do not turn.
Round 1	Hdc in ring 8 times, join with a slip stitch to first hdc, ch 1. *You now have* 8 hdc.
Round 2	2 hdc in each hdc to end of round, join with a slip stitch to first hdc, ch 1. *You now have* 16 hdc.
Round 3	* 1 hdc in first stitch, 2 hdc in next stitch; repeat from * to end of round, join with a slip stitch to first hdc, ch 1. *You now have* 24 hdc.
Round 4	* 1 hdc in first 2 stitches, 2 hdc in next stitch; repeat from * to end of round, join with a slip stitch to first hdc, ch 1. *You now have* 32 hdc.
Round 5	* 1 hdc in first 3 stitches, 2 hdc in next stitch; repeat from * to end of round, join with a slip stitch to first hdc, ch 1. *You now have* 40 hdc.
Round 6	1 hdc in each stitch to end of round, join with a slip stitch to first hdc. Change to CA, ch 1.
Round 7	* 1 hdc in first 4 stitches, 1 hdc in next stitch, 1 dc in round below; repeat from * to end of round, join with a slip stitch to first hdc, ch 1. *You now have* 48 sts.
Rounds 8 and 9	1 hdc in each stitch to end of round, join with a slip stitch to first hdc, ch 1.
Round 10	1 hdc in each stitch to end of round, join with a slip stitch to first hdc. Change to CB, ch 1.

Round 11	* 1 hdc in first 5 stitches, 1 hdc in next stitch, 1 dc in round below; repeat from * to end of round, join with a slip stitch to first hdc, ch 1. *You now have* 56 sts.
Rounds 12–14	1 hdc in each stitch to end of round, join with a slip stitch to first hdc. Change to CC, ch 1.
Round 15	* 1 hdc in first 4 stitches, 1 hdc in next stitch and 1 dc in round below; repeat from * to end of round, join with a slip stitch to first hdc, ch 1.
Round 16	1 hdc in each stitch to end of round, join with a slip stitch to first hdc.
	Draw yarn through last stitch to fasten off, and break yarn.
CROCHETING THE EARFLAP	
NOTE	The Earflaps are crocheted in rows. For hdc2tog, see page 59.
Row 1	Join CC right after the seam, ch 1, 1 hdc in the first 12 stitches, turn.
Row 2	Ch 1, hdc2tog, 1 hdc in next 8 stitches, hdc2tog, turn.
Row 3	Ch 1, hdc2tog, 1 hdc in next 6 stitches, hdc2tog, turn.
Row 4	Ch 1, 1 hdc in each stitch to end of row, turn.
Row 5	Ch 1, hdc2tog, 1 hdc in next 2 stitches, hdc2tog, turn.
Row 6	Ch 1, 1 hdc in each stitch to end of row, turn.
Row 7	Ch 1, hdc2tog twice.
	Draw yarn through last stitch to fasten off, then break yarn.
	Skip 13 stitches and join CC. Repeat Rows 1–7 for second Earflap.

	FINISHING
	Cut six 15" (37.5 cm) lengths of each color yarn.
	Align three lengths of each color (12 lengths in all), and tie an overhand knot at one end. Make a braid using four assorted-color strands for each group.
	Thread the unknotted end of the braid through the large-eye yarn needle. Attach the braid to the lower edge of one earflap on the wrong side by weaving the ends back and forth several times through the stitches. Avoid allowing the stitching yarns to show on the front of the earflap.
	Repeat for the other earflap.
	Weave loose ends into back of hat.

MAKING A FOUR-STRAND BRAID

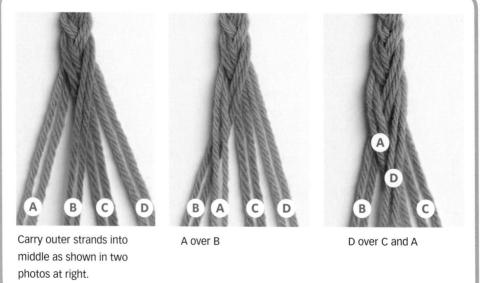

Carry outer strands into middle as shown in two photos at right.

A over B

D over C and A

OTHER YARNS TO TRY

Rowan Wool Cotton, 50% merino wool/50% cotton, 3.5 oz (50 g)/124 yds (113 m): (from top to bottom) 1 strand Antique #900 knit together with 1 strand August #953; 2 strands August; 1 strand Antique knit together with 1 strand Laurel #960; 2 strands Laurel

Pearl-Beaded Cap

No need to sacrifice style for comfort with this all-over beaded cap. Soft yarn combined with luminescent beads makes the cap a real show stopper. Once you get started, the rhythm of crocheting this hat will win you over to the technique and you won't want to stop.

Finished measurement
21" (53.3 cm) circumference

Yarn
Sport-weight yarn, 1 ball of off-white
I used Nashua June, 100% microfiber, 1¾ oz (50 g)/120 yds (110 m)
White #0001, 1 ball

Hook
US G/6 (4 or 4.25 mm), *or size you need to obtain correct gauge*

Gauge
18 sts and 16 rows = 4" × 4" (10 cm × 10 cm) in stitch pattern

Other supplies
Large-eye yarn needle
1 package of at least 450 colored glass beads, ⅛" (3 mm): size 6/0

Abbreviations
ch = chain
dc = double crochet
hdc = half double crochet
sc = single crochet
sts = stitches
yo = yarn over

STRING ME ALONG

Before you begin to crochet, you need to string the beads onto your yarn. Because the project takes approximately 450 beads, it would be difficult to string them all onto yarn at once. I suggest that you string on about 90 beads, then end the yarn when you need to add more beads; string another group before beginning again. (For more on working with beads, see page 13.)

CROCHETING THE HAT	
NOTE	This entire hat is worked back and forth in rows, then joined at the end of each row to form a round.
SET UP	Ch 4, join with a slip stitch to form a ring.
Round 1	Ch 1, work 18 hdc into ring, join with a slip st to first hdc, turn.
Row 2 (wrong side)	Ch 1, * sc in next stitch, pull up a bead, ch 1, skip 1; repeat from * to end of row, join with a slip stitch to first sc, turn. *You now have 16 stitches (counting the ch-1 spaces).*
Row 3	Ch 1, * work 2 hdc in each stitch and ch-1 space behind the bead; repeat from * to end of row, join with a slip stitch to first stitch, turn. *You now have 32 sts.*
Row 4 and all even-numbered rows	Ch 1, * sc in next stitch, pull up a bead, ch 1, skip 1; repeat from * to end of row, join with a slip stitch to first stitch, turn.
Row 5	Ch 1, * hdc in next stitch or ch-1 space, 2 hdc in next stitch; repeat from * to end of row, join with a slip stitch to first stitch, turn. *You now have 48 sts.*
Row 7	Ch 1, * hdc in next 2 stitches, 2 hdc in next stitch; repeat from * to end of row, join with a slip stitch to first stitch, turn. *You now have 64 sts.*

Row 9	Ch 1, * hdc in next 3 stitches, 2 hdc in next stitch; repeat from * to end of row, join with a slip stitch to first stitch, turn. *You now have* 80 sts.
Row 11	Ch 1, * hdc in next 4 stitches, 2 hdc in next stitch; repeat from * to end of row, join with a slip stitch to first stitch, turn. *You now have* 96 sts.
Row 13 and all odd-numbered rows to Row 31	Ch 1, hdc in each stitch to end of row, join with a slip stitch to first stitch, turn.
Row 32	Ch 1, * sc in next stitch, skip 1, work shell (dc, yo, pull through 2 loops, yo, pull up bead, pull through 2 loops, dc), skip 1; repeat from * to end of row, join with a slip stitch to first stitch.
FINISHING	
	Draw yarn through last stitch to fasten off, then break yarn. Weave loose ends into wrong side of hat.

ANOTHER YARN TO TRY

Nashua June, 100% microfiber, 1.75 oz (50 g)/120 yds (110 m): Bluebell #006

Faux-Suede Helmet

Snuggle up your ears in this cozy helmet that is all the rage. The remarkably realistic suede yarn combined with the soft trim will bring out your inner "sherpa." So easy in a basic half double crochet even a beginner would be up to the challenge.

Finished measurement
23" (58.4 cm) circumference

Yarn
Light worsted-weight ribbon-type suede yarn, 1 ball of tan
Heavy-weight plush-type yarn, 1 ball of cream
I used
MC = Berroco Suede, 100% nylon, 1¾ oz (50 g)/120 yds (111 m)
Hopalong Cassidy #3714, 2 balls
CC = Berroco Plush, 100% nylon, 1¾ oz (50 g), 90 yds (83 m)
Crema #1901, 1 ball

Hooks
For MC: US H/8 (5 mm), *or size you need to obtain correct gauge*
For CC: US I/9 (5.5 mm), *or size you need to obtain correct gauge*

Gauge
12 sts and 9 rows = 4" × 4" (10 cm × 10 cm) in hdc using MC

Other supplies
Large-eye yarn needle

Abbreviations
ch = chain
hdc = half double crochet
hdc2tog = half double crochet 2 together (see page 59)

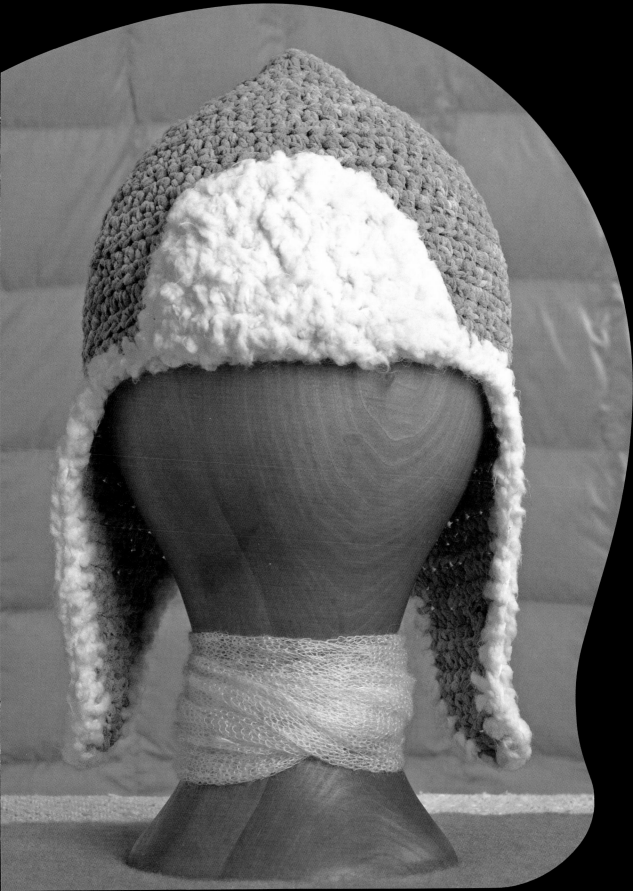

CROCHETING THE HELMET	
NOTE	At the end of each round, join with a slip stitch to first stitch and turn.
SET UP	With MC and H/8 (5mm) hook, ch 4, join with a slip stitch to form a ring.
Round 1	Ch 1, 8 hdc into ring, join with a slip stitch to ch-1.
Round 2	Ch 1, 2 hdc in each hdc to end of round, join with a slip stitch to ch-1. *You now have* 16 hdc.
Round 3	Ch 1, * 2 hdc in first stitch, hdc in next stitch; repeat from * to end of round, join with a slip stitch to ch-1. *You now have* 24 hdc.
Round 4	Ch 1, * 1 hdc in next 2 stitches, 2 hdc in next stitch; repeat from * to end of round, join with a slip stitch to ch-1. *You now have* 32 hdc.
Round 5	Ch 1, * 1 hdc in next 3 stitches, 2 hdc in next stitch; repeat from * to end of round, join with a slip stitch to ch-1. *You now have* 40 hdc.
Round 6	Ch 1, * 1 hdc in next 4 stitches, 2 hdc in next stitch; repeat from * to end of round, join with a slip stitch to ch-1. *You now have* 48 hdc.
Round 7	Ch 1, * 1 hdc in next 5 stitches, 2 hdc in next stitch; repeat from * to end of round, join with a slip stitch to ch-1. *You now have* 56 hdc.
Round 8	Ch 1, * 1 hdc in next 6 stitches, 2 hdc in next stitch; repeat from * to end of round, join with a slip stitch to ch-1. *You now have* 64 hdc.
Round 9	Ch 1, * 1 hdc in next 7 stitches, 2 hdc in next stitch; repeat from * to end of round, join with a slip stitch to ch-1. *You now have* 72 hdc.
Rounds 11–17	Ch 1, * hdc in each stitch; repeat from * to end of round, join with a slip stitch to ch-1.
SHAPING THE CROWN	
Row 1	Ch 1, 1 hdc in next 46 stitches, turn.

A DECREASE METHOD: HDC2TOG

I know the abbreviation "hdc2tog" looks suspiciously like something from Chemistry 101, but it's actually a way of decreasing in crochet. Although the slip stitch is often used to decrease, this pattern calls for you to "half double crochet 2 together (hdc2tog)." Here's how it's done:

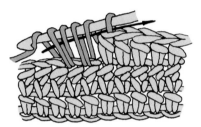

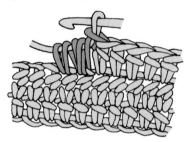

1. (Yo, insert hook in next stitch and draw up a loop) twice.

2. Yo and draw the yarn through all 5 loops on the hook.

Row 2	Ch 1, hdc2tog, 1 hdc in next 42 stitches, hdc2tog, turn. *You now have 44 hdc.*
Rows 3, 5, and 7	Ch 1, 1 hdc in each stitch to end of row, turn.
Row 4	Ch 1, hdc2tog, 1 hdc in next 40 stitches, hdc2tog, turn. *You now have 42 hdc.*
Row 6	Ch 1, hdc2tog, 1 hdc in next 38 stitches, hdc2tog, turn. *You now have 40 hdc.*
CROCHETING THE EARFLAPS	
Row 1	Ch 1, 1 hdc in next 12 stitches, turn. (*Note:* For the next eight rows, work on these stitches only, decreasing as indicated.)

Row 2	Ch 1, hdc2tog, 1 hdc in next 8 stitches, hdc2tog, turn.
Rows 3, 5, 7 and 9	Ch 1, 1 hdc in each stitch to end of row, turn.
Row 4	Ch 1, hdc2tog, 1 hdc in next 6 stitches, hdc2tog, turn.
Row 6	Ch 1, hdc2tog, 1 hdc in next 4 stitches, hdc2tog, turn.
Row 8	Ch 1, hdc2tog, 1 hdc in next 2 stitches, hdc2tog, turn.
	Draw yarn through last stitch to fasten off, then break yarn.
	Skip next 16 stitches and join yarn. Working over the next 12 stitches, repeat Rows 1–9 for second Earflap.
FINISHING	
	Using the I/9 (5.5 mm) hook and CC, join yarn to the edge at the back of the left earflap, then hdc in each stitch around hat.
	Draw yarn through last stitch to fasten off, then break yarn. Weave loose ends into back of hat.
CROCHETING THE CENTER FRONT FLAP	
SET UP	Using the I/9 (5.5 mm) hook and CC, ch 13; 1 hdc in second chain from the hook and in each remaining chain, turn. *You now have 12 hdc.*
Row 1	Ch 1, hdc2tog, 1 hdc in next 8 stitches, hdc2tog, turn. *You now have 10 hdc.*
Row 2	Ch 1, 1 hdc in each stitch to end of row, turn.
Row 3	Ch 1, hdc2tog, 1 hdc in next 6 stitches, hdc2tog, turn. *You now have 8 hdc.*

Row 4	Ch 1, hdc2tog, 1 hdc in next 4 stitches, hdc2tog, turn. *You now have 6 hdc.*
Row 5	Ch 1, 1 hdc in each stitch to end of row, turn.
Row 6	Ch 1, hdc2tog, 1 hdc in next 2 stitches, hdc2tog, turn. *You now have 4 hdc.*
	Draw yarn through last stitch to fasten off, then break yarn.

SEWING THE FLAP TO THE HELMET FRONT

Using CC, attach Front Flap to the right side of the helmet at the center front by stitching around it on all sides. Weave loose ends into inside of hat.

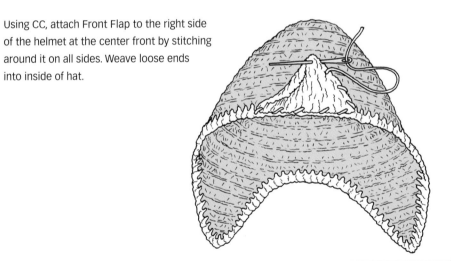

Colorful Sun Hat

Cheerful spots of color transform a practical sun hat into this stylish work of art. Using a double strand of crochet cotton, you'll have this hat done in a jiffy. Try a few other color combos for completely different looks.

Finished measurement
21½" (54.6 cm) circumference

Yarn
Sport-weight cotton yarn: 3 balls of teal; 1 ball each of lavender, yellow, green, and plum

I used Royale 3 Fashion Crochet Thread, 100% mercerized cotton, 150 yds (137 m)
MC: Warm Teal #0065, 3 balls
CA: Warm Blue #0175, 1 ball
CB: Light Yellow Green #2236, 1 ball
CC: Plum #0871, 1 ball

Hook
US H/8 (5 mm), *or size you need to obtain correct gauge*

Gauge
15 sts and 11 rounds = 4" × 4" (10 cm × 10 cm) in hdc, with yarn doubled
Note: All yarns are used double throughout.

Other supplies
Large-eye yarn needle
Stitch markers

Abbreviations
ch = chain
hdc = half double crochet
sc = single crochet

CROCHETING THE HAT

NOTE	At the end of each round, join with a slip stitch, but do not turn.
SET UP	With 2 strands of MC, beginning at center top of hat, ch 4, join with a slip stitch in first chain to form a ring.
Round 1 (right side)	Ch 2 (counts as hdc), 11 hdc in ring, join to top of ch-2. Mark for right side. *You now have* 12 hdc.
Round 2	Ch 2 (counts as hdc), hdc in same stitch as joining, * 2 hdc in next stitch; repeat from * to end of round, join to top of ch-2. *You now have* 24 hdc.
Round 3	Ch 2, * 2 hdc in next stitch, hdc in next 2 stitches; repeat from * to end of round, join to top of ch-2. *You now have* 32 hdc.
Round 4	Ch 2, * 2 hdc in next stitch, hdc in next 3 stitches; repeat from * to end of round, join to top of ch-2. *You now have* 40 hdc.
Round 5	Ch 2, * 2 hdc in next stitch, hdc in next 4 stitches; repeat from * to end of round, join to top of ch-2. *You now have* 48 hdc.
Round 6	Ch 2, * 2 hdc in next stitch, hdc in next 5 stitches; repeat from * to end of round, join to top of ch-2. *You now have* 56 hdc.
Round 7	Ch 2, * 2 hdc in next stitch, hdc in next 6 stitches; repeat from * to end of round, join to top of ch-2. *You now have* 64 hdc.
Round 8	Ch 2, * 2 hdc in next stitch, hdc in next 7 stitches; repeat from * to end of round, join to top of ch-2. *You now have* 72 hdc.
Round 9	Ch 2, * 2 hdc in next stitch, hdc in next 8 stitches; repeat from * to end of round, join to top of ch-2. *You now have* 80 hdc.
Round 10	Ch 2, hdc in each stitch to end of round, join to top of ch-2.

Next Rounds	Repeat Round 10 until piece measures 5" (12.7 cm) from center top.
CROCHETING THE COLOR ROUNDS	
SET UP	Drop MC (but do not break); join 2 strands of CA with a slip stitch in same stitch as joining stitch.
Round 1	Ch 1, * sc in next stitch, ch 1, skip 1 stitch; repeat from * to end of round, join with a slip stitch in top of ch-1. Draw yarn through last stitch to fasten off CA, and pick up MC.
Rounds 2 and 3	With MC, ch 1, * sc in next ch-1 space, ch 1; repeat from * to end of round, join with a slip stitch in top of ch-1. Drop MC (but do not break), join 2 strands of CB with a slip stitch in same stitch as joining stitch.
Round 4	Ch 1, * sc in first stitch, ch 1, skip 1 stitch; repeat from * to end of round, join with a slip stitch in top of ch-1. Draw yarn through last stitch to fasten off CB, and pick up MC.
Round 5	With MC, ch 1, * sc in next ch-1 space, ch 1; repeat from * to end of round, join with a slip stitch in top of ch-1.
CROCHETING THE BRIM	
SET UP	Place a marker to mark beginning of rounds for Brim. *Note:* The rounds may not work out exactly, but simply begin each new round when you reach the marker.
Round 1	Continuing with 2 strands of MC, ch 1, * (sc in next ch-1 space, ch 1) twice, (sc, ch 1, sc) in next ch-1 space; repeat from * to end of round, join with a slip stitch in top of ch-1.
Round 2	Ch 1, * (sc, ch 1, sc) in next ch-1 space, (ch 1, sc in next ch-1 space) 5 times; repeat from * to end of round, join with a slip stitch in top of ch-1.

	Drop MC (but do not break); join 2 strands of CC with a slip stitch in same stitch as joining stitch.
Round 3	With CC, ch 1, * (sc, ch 1, sc) in next ch-1 space, (ch 1, sc in next ch-1 space) 6 times; repeat from * to end of round, join with a slip stitch in top of ch-1. Draw yarn through to fasten off CC, and pick up MC.
Round 4	With MC, ch 1, * (sc, ch 1, sc) in next ch-1 space, (ch 1, sc in next ch-1 space) 9 times; repeat from * to end of round, join with a slip stitch in top of ch-1.
Round 5	Ch 1, * (sc, ch 1, sc) in next ch-1 space, (ch 1, sc in next ch-1 space) 10 times; repeat from * to end of round, join with a slip stitch in top of ch-1. Drop MC (but do not break), join 2 strands of CB with a slip stitch in same stitch as joining stitch.
Round 6	With CB, ch 1, (sc in next ch-1 space, ch 1) in each ch-1 space to end of round, join with a slip stitch in top of ch-1. Draw yarn through to fasten off CB, and pick up MC.
Rounds 7 and 8	With MC, ch 1, (sc in next ch-1 space, ch 1) in each ch-1 space to end of round, join with a slip stitch in top of ch-1. Drop MC (but do not break); join 2 strands of CA with a slip stitch in same stitch as joining stitch.
Round 9	With CA, ch 1, (sc in next ch-1 space, ch 1) in each ch-1 space to end of round, join with a slip stitch in top of ch-1. Draw yarn through to fasten off CA, and pick up MC.
Round 10	With MC, ch 1, (sc in next ch-1 space, ch 1) in each ch-1 space around, join with a slip stitch in top of ch-1, turn.
Round 11	Ch 1, working in front loops only, slip stitch in each stitch to end of round, join with a slip stitch in top of ch-1.
	Draw yarn through last stitch to fasten off, then break yarn.

FINISHING	
	Weave loose ends into wrong side of hat.

OTHER YARNS TO TRY

Nashua June, 100% microfiber, 1.75 oz (50 g)/120 yds (110 m): 1 strand Ivory #002 knit together with 1 strand willow #005; 2 strands Periwinkle #007

Fair Isle Hat

Classic Fair Isle is updated in the trendy colors of this hat. Try it out on a ski slope or on a shopping trip — it will surely keep the chill at bay. The crochet rib is worked separately and then added later.

Finished measurement
22" (55.9 cm) circumference

Yarn
Worsted-weight yarn in yellow green, natural, black, and light teal: 1 ball each
I used Nashua Handknits Julia, 50% wool/ 25% kid mohair/25% alpaca, 93 yds (85 m)/ 1.75 oz (50 g)
CA = Lady's Mantle #3961, 1 ball
CB = Natural #0010, 1 ball
CC = Forged Iron #0050, 1 ball
CD = Blue Thyme #4936, 1 ball

Hook
US H/8 (5 mm), *or size you need to obtain correct gauge*

Gauge
13 sts and 12 rows = 4" × 4" (10 cm × 10 cm) in hdc

Other supplies
Large-eye yarn needle

Abbreviations
ch = chain
hdc = half double crochet
sc = single crochet

CROCHETING THE HAT	
SET UP	Beginning at lower edge, with CA, chain 69. Hdc in second chain from hook and in each chain to end of row; turn. *You now have* 68 hdc.
Rows 1–4	Ch 1, hdc in each stitch to end of row, turn.
Row 5	Ch 1, * 3 hdc CA, 1 hdc CB; repeat from * to end of row; break CA, turn.
Row 6	Using CB, ch 1, hdc to end of row, turn. Join CD.
Row 7	Ch 1, 2 hdc CB, *1 hdc CD, 3 hdc CB; repeat from * to last stitch, end 1 hdc CB, turn.
Row 8	Ch 1, * 3 hdc CD, 1 hdc CB; repeat from * to end of row, turn.
Row 9	Repeat Row 7. Drop CD.
Row 10	Repeat Row 6. Pick up CD.
Row 11	Ch 1, * 1 hdc CD, 3 hdc CB; repeat from * to end of row, turn.
Row 12	Ch 1, 1 hdc CD, *1 hdc CB, 3 hdc CD; repeat from * to last 2 stitches, end 2 hdc CD, turn.
Row 13	Repeat Row 11. Break CD; join CC.
Row 14	Ch 1, 1 hdc CB, * 1 hdc CC, 3 hdc CB; repeat from * to last 2 stitches, end 2 hdc CB, turn. Break CB.
Rows 15–22	Using CC, ch 1, hdc to end of row, turn.
DECREASING FOR THE CROWN	
NOTE	For how to decrease by crocheting 2 stitches together in half double crochet, see page 59.

Row 1	Ch 1, * hdc in next 2 stitches, hdc next 2 stitches together; repeat from * to end of row, turn.
Row 2	Ch 1, * hdc in next stitch, hdc 2 together; repeat from * to end of row.
	Draw yarn through last stitch to fasten off, then break yarn.

CROCHETING THE RIBBING

Set Up	Using CA, chain 12. Sc in second stitch from hook and in each stitch to end of row, turn. *You now have* 11 sc.
Row 1	Working in the back loop only, ch 1, sc in each stitch to end of row, turn.
Next Rows	Repeat Row 1 until piece measures approximately 21" (52.5 cm) from the beginning. Draw yarn through last stitch to fasten off, then break yarn.

FINISHING

	Sew side seam on hat and on ribbing. Thread a large-eye needle with matching yarn and run a line of stitches along the top edge; draw up the thread to close the hole.
	Pin the ribbing to the lower edge, aligning seams and stretching it slightly to fit; sew in place. Turn ribbing up to form a cuff at lower edge of hat.
	Weave in any loose ends.

Angora & Diamonds

Soft and slouchy is the magic combination for this hat. With the bunny-soft angora-blend yarn, you'll never want to take it off. The hat is crocheted in a simple rectangle, then the diamond pattern is worked over the surface before you stitch up the back seam.

Finished measurement
21½" (54.6 cm) circumference

Yarn
Worsted-weight angora-type yarn, 2 skeins of periwinkle blue
I used Classic Elite Lush, 50% angora/50% wool, 1¾ oz (50 g)/124 yds (113 m) Thistle #4407, 2 skeins

Hook
H/8 (5 mm), *or size you need to obtain correct gauge*

Gauge
14 sts and 18 rows = 4" × 4" (10 cm × 10 cm) in sc

Other supplies
Large-eye yarn needle
Elastic thread, 1 package in color to match yarn

Abbreviations
ch = chain
sc = single crochet

	CROCHETING THE HAT
NOTE	This hat is worked flat, back and forth in rows, then joined together in a seam at the back and gathered at the top to form a hat.
SET UP	Chain 75.
Row 1	Sc in second chain from hook and in each chain across; turn. *You now have 74 sc.*
Row 2	Ch 1, sc in each sc across; turn.
Next Rows	Repeat Row 2 until piece measures 6" (15 cm). *You now have 26 rows.*
	Draw yarn through last stitch to fasten off, then break yarn.
	CROCHETING THE RIBBING
NOTE	Ribbing is worked as a separate piece, then sewn on to the hat.
SET UP	Chain 5.
Row 1	Sc in second chain from hook and in each chain across; turn. *You now have 4 sc.*
Row 2	Ch 1, sc in back loop only of each sc across; turn.
Next Rows	Repeat Row 2 until piece measures 20" (50 cm).
	Draw yarn through last stitch to fasten off, then break yarn.
	CROCHETING THE DIAMOND PATTERN
	Starting in the lower right-hand corner of the hat, one stitch in from the side edge, join the yarn with a slip stitch; work a chain stitch across 1 stitch, then chain stitch across the stitch on the next row up and to the left of the first stitch (on the diagonal).

	Continue in this manner until you reach the top of the hat. Draw the yarn through the last stitch to fasten off, then break yarn.
	Return to the lower edge of the hat, skip eight stitches from where you began the first diagonal and work another diagonal in the same manner, parallel to the first, from the lower edge to the top of the hat.
	Continue in this manner until you have worked a diagonal beginning in every ninth stitch. One stitch remains before the left-hand side edge. You have worked eight diagonal lines from the lower edge to the top of hat.
	Starting in the lower left-hand corner of the hat, work eight diagonal lines, crossing over the first set of lines in the opposite direction, to create the diamond pattern.

FINISHING

	Use mattress stitch to sew the back seam on hat (see page 30).
	Pin ribbing to bottom edge of hat, easing it to fit evenly all around, then use mattress stitch to sew ribbing to hat.
	Using elastic thread, make a line of running stitches on the wrong side of the ribbing just inside the bottom edge. Take care to work so that the stitching does not show on the right side of the ribbing. Make another line of elastic running stitches on the wrong side of the ribbing about 3 rows away from the first.
	To gather top of hat, weave a length of matching yarn through every other stitch along top edge, then pull tight and tie a secure knot.
	Cut a 3" (7.5 cm) square of cardboard, and make a pompom, following the instructions on page 15. Use the tails of the tying yarn to attach the pompom to the top of the hat. Weave loose ends into wrong side of hat.

Retro Flowers

Flash back to a bygone era with this fun retro cap. A garland of flowers that cascades down the side makes the simple double crochet cap sparkle. This cap is so easy you'll want to make one for every occasion.

Finished measurement
20" (50.8 cm) circumference

Yarn
Sport-weight sparkle yarn, 1 ball each of burgundy and red
I used Paton's Brilliant, 69% acrylic/31% polyester, 1¾ oz (50 g)/166 yds (152 m)
MC = Beautiful Burgundy #4430, 1 ball
CC = Radiant Red #4942, 1 ball

Hook
US G/6 (4 or 4.25 mm), *or size you need to obtain correct gauge*

Gauge
19 sts and 8 rows = 4" × 4" (10 cm × 10 cm) in dc

Other supplies
Large-eye yarn needle
Stitch marker

Abbreviations
ch = chain
dc = double crochet
hdc = half double crochet
sc = single crochet
sts = stitches
yo = yarn over

CROCHETING THE CAP	
SET UP	Using MC, ch 4, join with a slip stitch in first chain to form a ring.
NOTE	At the end of each round, join with a slip stitch in the top of the ch-3; do not turn.
Round 1 (right side)	Ch 3, 11 dc in ring, join with a slip stitch in top of ch-3. Mark this as the right side. *You now have* 12 dc (the beginning ch 3 counts as 1 dc).
Round 2	Ch 3, 1 dc in base of ch-3, (2 dc in next dc) to end of round, join with a slip stitch in ch-3. *You now have* 24 sts.
Round 3	Ch 3, (2 dc in next dc, 1 dc in next dc) to end of round, join with a slip stitch in ch-3. *You now have* 36 sts.
Round 4	Ch 3, (2 dc in next dc, 1 dc in next 2 dc) to end of round, join with a slip stitch in ch-3. *You now have* 48 sts.
Round 5	Ch 3, (2 dc in next dc, 1 dc in next 3 dc) to end of round, join with a slip stitch in ch-3. *You now have* 60 sts.
Round 6	Ch 3, (2 dc in next dc, 1 dc in next 4 dc) to end of round, join with a slip stitch in ch-3. *You now have* 72 sts.
Round 7	Ch 3, (2 dc in next dc, 1 dc in next 5 dc) to end of round, join with a slip stitch in ch-3. *You now have* 84 sts.
Round 8	Ch 3, (2 dc in next dc, 1 dc in next 6 dc) to end of round, join with a slip stitch in ch-3. *You now have* 96 sts.
Next Rounds	Dc in each stitch to end of each round until cap measures approximately 6" (15 cm) or desired length from top.
	Draw yarn through last stitch to fasten off, then break yarn. Weave loose ends into back of hat.

CROCHETING THE FLOWERS	
NOTE	The three patterns that follow are for double flowers with varying widths at the center, depending on whether you work single crochet, half double crochet, or double crochet into the beginning ring. In the photo, notice that two of the flowers use MC for the petals and CC for the flower center, and three are the reverse. Make as many flowers as you wish. If you'd like to have some single flowers in the mix, follow the directions for any of the doubles, but stop at the end of Round 2 and omit Round 3. These flowers make fabulous ornaments for other knitted or crocheted items, or you can even attach a jewelry pin to the back so that you can easily move them from one outfit to another. Enjoy!
NOTE	When you break the yarn for each flower, leave a 6" (15 cm) tail for sewing the flower to the cap.
Flower 1 (Single Crochet Center)	
SET UP	Ch 4, join with a slip stitch in first chain to form a ring.
Round 1	Ch 1, 12 sc in ring, join with a slip stitch to beginning ch-1. *You now have 12 sc.*
Round 2	Ch 1, working in back loops only, (1 sc, ch 4, 1 sc) in each sc to end of round, join with a slip stitch to beginning ch-1.
Round 3	Ch 1, working in front loops of Round 1 only, (1 sc, ch 4, 1 sc) in each sc to end of round, join with a slip stitch to beginning ch-1.
	Draw yarn through last stitch to fasten off, then break yarn.
Flower 2 (Half Double Crochet Center)	
SET UP	Ch 4, join with a slip stitch in first chain to form a ring.
Round 1	Ch 2, 12 hdc in ring, join with a slip stitch to beginning ch-1. *You now have 12 hdc.*

Round 2	Ch 1, working in back loops only, (1 hdc, ch 4, 1 hdc) in each hdc to end of round, join with a slip stitch to beginning ch-1.
Round 3	Ch 1, working in front loops of Round 1 only, (1 sc, ch 4, 1 sc) in each hdc to end of round, join with a slip stitch to beginning ch-1.
	Draw yarn through last stitch to fasten off, then break yarn.
Flower 3 (Double Crochet Center)	
SET UP	Ch 4, join with a slip stitch in first chain to form a ring.
Round 1	Ch 3, 12 dc in ring, join with a slip stitch to beginning ch-1. *You now have* 12 dc.
Round 2	Ch 1, working in back loops only, (1 dc, ch 4, 1 dc) in each dc around, join with a slip stitch to beginning ch-1.
Round 3	Ch 1, working in front loops of Round 1 only, (1 sc, ch 4, 1 sc) in each dc around, join with a slip stitch to beginning ch-1.
	Draw yarn through last stitch to fasten off, then break yarn.
CROCHETING THE FLOWER CENTERS	
SET UP	With MC or CC, ch 3, * yo, insert hook into first chain and pull through two loops; repeat from * four more times.
	Yo, pull through all six loops on hook. Draw yarn through last stitch to fasten off, then break yarn, leaving a 6" (15 cm) tail.
FINISHING	
	Weave loose ends into back of hat. Arrange flowers on cap as shown in photo and use the yarn tails to stitch them into place, see page 94.

OTHER YARNS TO TRY

(flowers only)

Patons Brilliant, 69% acrylic/19% nylon/12% polyester, 1.75 oz (50 g)/166 yds (152 m): #03314 Lilac Luster and #0308 Crystal Cream

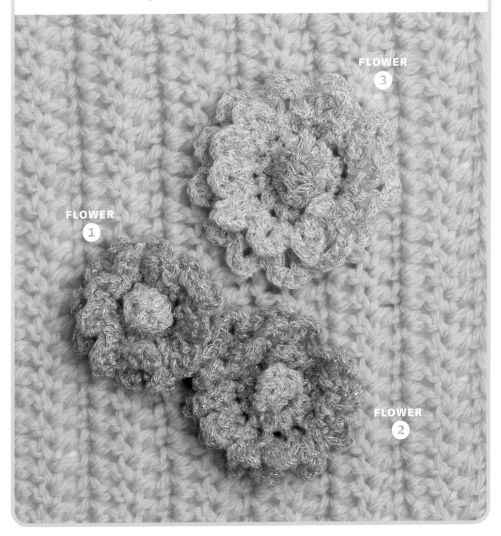

Gold-Chain Juliet

Make a dazzling entrance in this metallic gold cap. Super simple in a very basic single crochet, it's the yarn that does all the work. Get in touch with your inner "Juliet" and make your Romeo swoon.

Finished measurement
22" (55.9 cm) circumference

Yarn
Fingering-weight metallic-type yarn, 2 balls of gold
I used Lion Brand Lamé Metallic Yarn, fingering weight, 35% metalized polyester/ 65% rayon, 56 oz (19 g)/75 yds (68.6 m) Gold #170, 2 cones

Hooks
US H/8 (5 mm) and G/6 (4 or 4.25 mm), *or sizes you need to obtain correct gauge*

Gauge
19 sts and 22 rounds = 4" × 4" (10 cm × 10 cm) in sc (with larger hook)

Other supplies
Split-ring stitch marker
Large-eye yarn needle

Abbreviations
ch = chain
sc = single crochet
sts = stitches

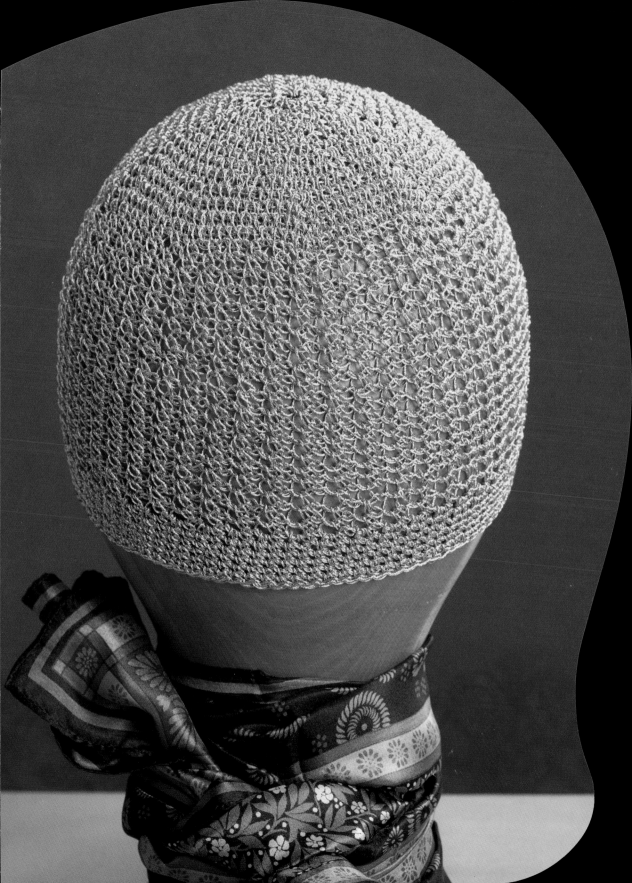

CROCHETING THE CAP	
NOTE	At the end of each round in this section, join with a slip stitch, but do not turn.
SET UP	With larger hook, ch 4, join with a slip stitch to first chain to form a ring.
Round 1 (right side)	Ch 1, sc in ring 8 times, slip stitch in ch-1 to join. *You now have* 8 sc.
Round 2	Ch 1, 2 sc in each sc around, slip stitch in ch-1 to join. *You now have* 16 sc.
Round 3	Ch 1, (2 sc in next sc, 1 sc in next sc) 8 times, slip stitch in ch-1 to join. *You now have* 24 sts.
Round 4	Ch 1, (2 sc in next sc, 1 sc in next 2 sc) 8 times, slip stitch in ch-1 to join. *You now have* 32 sts.
Round 5	Ch 1, (2 sc in next sc, 1 sc in next 3 stitches) 8 times, slip stitch in ch-1 to join. *You now have* 40 sts.
Round 6	Ch 1, (2 sc in next sc, 1 sc in next 4 sc) 8 times. *You now have* 48 sts.
Round 7	Ch 1, (2 sc in next sc, 1 sc in next 5 sc) 8 times. *You now have* 56 sts.
Round 8	Ch 1, (2 sc in next sc, 1 sc in next 6 sc) 8 times. *You now have* 64 sts.
Round 9	Ch 1, (2 sc in next sc, 1 sc in next 7 sc) 8 times. *You now have* 72 sts.
Round 10	Ch 1, (2 sc in next sc, 1 sc in next 8 sc) 8 times. *You now have* 80 sts.
Round 11	Ch 1, (2 sc in next sc, 1 sc in next 9 sc) 8 times. *You now have* 88 sts.
Round 12	Ch 1, (2 sc in next sc, 1 sc in next 10 sc) 8 times. *You now have* 96 sts.
Round 13	Ch 1, (2 sc in next sc, 1 sc in next 11 sc) 8 times. *You now have* 104 sts.

Round 14	Ch 1, 1 sc in same stitch as joining, (ch 1, skip 1 sc, 1 sc in next sc) to end of round, ending last repeat with slip stitch in beginning ch-1. Place a marker on this round.
Round 15	Ch 1, (1 sc in sc, ch 1, skip ch-1) to end of round.
Next Rounds	Repeat Round 15 until cap measures 4" (10 cm) from Round 14.
CROCHETING THE BAND	
NOTE	In this section, join and turn at the end of each round.
Round 1	With smaller hook, sc in each sc to end of round, join, turn, ch 1.
Rounds 2–6	Repeat Round 1.
Round 7	Slip stitch loosely in each sc around. Draw yarn through last stitch to fasten off, then cut yarn.
FINISHING	
	Weave loose ends into back of hat.

Dressy Cloche

Show some fashion flair with this smart cloche. Simple shaping and a woven-yarn detail make this no-fuss project a joy to work on. Try a different color combo to make it uniquely you.

Finished measurement
21" (53.3 cm) circumference

Yarn
Worsted-weight wool, 1 ball of black and 4 yds of off-white
I used Patons Classic Wool, 100% wool, 3½ oz (100 g)/223 yds (204 m)
MC: Black # 226, 1 ball
CC: Off-white, approximately 4 yds (3.6 m)

Hook
US H/8 (5 mm), *or size you need to obtain correct gauge*

Gauge
14 sts and 17 rows = 4" × 4" (10 cm × 10 cm) in sc

Other supplies
Large-eye yarn needle

Abbreviations
ch = chain
sc = single crochet

CROCHETING THE HAT	
NOTE	Join with a slip stitch at the end of each round, do not turn.
SET UP	Using MC, ch 4, join with a slip stitch to form a ring.
Round 1	Ch 1, work 8 sc into ring, join with a slip stitch to first sc.
Round 2	Ch 1, 2 sc in each sc to end of round, join with a slip stitch to first sc. *You now have* 16 sc.
Round 3	Ch 1, * sc in first stitch, 2 sc in next stitch; repeat from * to end of round, join with a slip stitch to first sc. *You now have* 24 sc.
Round 4	Ch 1, * sc in first 2 stitches, 2 sc in next stitch; repeat from * to end of round, join with a slip stitch to first sc. *You now have* 32 sc.
Rounds 5, 7, 9, 11 and 13	Ch 1, sc in each stitch to end of round, join with a slip stitch to first sc.
Round 6	Ch 1, * sc in first 3 stitches, 2 sc in next stitch; repeat from * to end of round, join with a slip stitch to first sc. *You now have* 40 sc.
Round 8	Ch 1, * sc in first 4 stitches, 2 sc in next stitch; repeat from * to end of round, join with a slip stitch to first sc. *You now have* 48 sc.
Round 10	Ch 1, * sc in first 5 stitches, 2 sc in next stitch; repeat from * to end of round, join with a slip stitch to first sc. *You now have* 56 sc.
Round 12	Ch 1, * sc in first 6 stitches, 2 sc in next stitch; repeat from * to end of round, join with a slip stitch to first sc. *You now have* 64 sc.
Round 14	Ch 1, * sc in first 7 stitches, 2 sc in next stitch; repeat from * to end of round, join with a slip stitch to first sc. *You now have* 72 sc.
Rounds 15–29	Ch 1, sc in each stitch to end of round, join with a slip stitch to first sc.

Round 30	Ch 1, working in front loop only, * sc in first 2 sc, 2 sc in next stitch; repeat from * to end of round, join with a slip stitch to first sc. *You now have* 96 sc.
Rounds 31–35	Ch 1, sc in each stitch to end of round, join with a slip stitch to first sc.
	Draw yarn through last stitch to fasten off, then break yarn. Weave loose ends into wrong side of hat.

STITCHING THE BAND

Cut four lengths of CC, each 55" (1.4 m) long. Thread the yarn through a large-eye yarn needle so that the yarn is doubled. Starting just above the increase for the brim, take the threaded needle under 2 crochet stitches, then over the next 2 crochet stitches all the way around the hat. Take care to keep these running stitches along the same round of single crochet stitches.

Repeat the running stitches on the next round above the first, but offset these stitches by weaving over the 2 stitches that you wove under on the previous round.

Repeat the line of running stitches for three more rounds, offsetting each from the round of stitches at right, as shown.

Weave loose ends into wrong side of hat.

Running stitches for band

Flower Child

Color-popping hues add plenty of verve to this oh-so-chic little girl's hat. It's worked in a basic half double crochet with a little added texture from a crochet around the post. Pop on a fun crochet flower to finish off the look. Any little girl would love to prance around with this perky hat.

Finished measurement
21" (53.3 cm) circumference

Yarn
Worsted-weight wool, 1 skein green and 1 skein pink
I used Cascade 220, 100% wool, 3.5 oz (100 g)/ 200 yds (201 m)
MC = 1 skein green #8903
CC = 1 skein pink #7804

Hook
US H/8 (5 mm), *or size you need to obtain correct gauge*

Gauge
14 sts and 9 rows = 4" × 4" (10 cm × 10 cm) in hdc

Other supplies
Large-eye yarn needle

Abbreviations
ch = chain
dc = double crochet
FPdc = front post double crochet (see Some Special Techniques on page 98)
hdc = half double crochet
sc = single crochet
sts = stitches

CROCHETING THE HAT	
NOTE	Join with a slip stitch in first stitch at the end of each round; do not turn.
SET UP	With MC, ch 4, join with a slip stitch to first ch-1 to form a ring.
Round 1	Ch 1, 8 hdc into ring, join to first hdc. *You now have* 8 hdc.
Round 2	Ch 1, 2 hdc in each hdc to end of round, join to first hdc. *You now have* 16 hdc.
Round 3	Ch 1, beginning in first hdc * 2 hdc in next hdc, hdc in next hdc, dc in hdc from previous round; repeat from * to end of round, join to first hdc. *You now have* 32 sts.
Round 4	Ch 1, * hdc in next 2 stitches, 2 hdc in next stitch, FPdc around dc of previous round; repeat from * to end of round, join to first hdc. *You now have* 40 sts.
Round 5	Ch 1, * hdc in next 4 stitches, FPdc around dc of previous round; repeat from * to end of round, join to first hdc.
Round 6	Ch 1, * hdc in next 2 stitches, work 2 hdc in next stitch, hdc in next stitch, FPdc around dc of previous round; repeat from * to end of round, join to first hdc. *You now have* 48 sts.
Round 7	Ch 1, * hdc in next 5 stitches, FPdc around dc of previous round; repeat from * to end of round, join to first hdc.
Round 8	Ch 1, * hdc in next 2 stitches, work 2 hdc in next stitch, hdc in next 2 stitches, FPdc around dc of previous round; repeat from * to end of round, join to first hdc. *You now have* 56 sts.
Rounds 9–15	Ch 1, * hdc in next 6 stitches, FPdc around dc of previous round; repeat from * to end of round, join to first hdc.

Round 16	Ch 1, working in front loops only, * (hdc in next stitch, work 2 hdc in next stitch) three times, FPdc around dc of previous round; repeat from * to end of round, join to first hdc. *You now have* 80 sts.
Round 17	Ch 1, * (hdc in next 2 stitches, work 2 hdc in next stitch) three times, FPdc around dc of previous round; repeat from * to end of round, join to first hdc. *You now have* 104 sts.
Rounds 18 and 19	Ch 1, * hdc in next 12 stitches, FPdc around dc of previous round; repeat from * to end of round, join to first hdc.
Round 20	Ch 1, * (hdc in next 5 stitches, work 2 hdc in next stitch) twice, FPdc around dc of previous round; repeat from * around, join to first hdc. *You now have* 120 sts.
	Draw yarn through last stitch to fasten off, then break yarn.
CROCHETING THE FLOWER	
Set Up	With CC, ch 4, join with a slip stitch to first ch to form a ring.
Round 1	Ch 2 (counts as sc), 11 sc into ring, end join with a slip stitch to beginning chain. *You now have* 12 sc (including the beginning ch-2).
Round 2	Ch 1, working in front loops only of Round 1, * (sc, ch 4, sc) in first sc and in each sc to end of round, join with a slip stitch to first sc. *You now have* 12 petals.
Round 3	Ch 1, working in back loops only of Round 1, beginning in first sc, * (sc, ch 6, sc) in next sc, (sc, ch 4, sc) in next sc; repeat from * to end of round, join to first sc.
	Draw yarn through last stitch to fasten off, then break yarn, leaving a 6" (15 cm) tail.

CROCHETING THE FLOWER CENTER

SET UP	With MC, ch 3, * yo, insert hook into first chain and pull through two loops; repeat from * four more times.
	Yo, pull through all six loops on hook. Draw yarn through last stitch to fasten off, then break yarn, leaving a 6" (15 cm) tail.

ATTACHING THE FLOWER

Thread yarn tail of Flower Center through a large-eye needle, and sew the center into the middle of the flower. Weave in loose ends.

Turn up the brim of the hat at center front (see illustration below). Thread yarn tail of Flower through a large-eye needle and use it to stitch the Flower to the hat, sewing through both brim and crown to keep brim in place against the crown of the hat.

Weave loose ends into wrong side of hat.

OTHER YARNS TO TRY

Cascade 220, 100% wool, 3.5 oz (100 g)/220 yds (201 m): Flower, Off White #8010 and Base, Peach #7804

Aran-Style Cables

Classic style and color create
the perfect aran hat. This hat's
a bit of a challenge, but who
doesn't like a little challenge once
in awhile! Besides I know you're
up to the task. Just take your time
and you'll get the hang of it.

Finished measurement
22" (55.8 cm) circumference

Yarn
Worsted-weight wool, 1 skein of off white
I used Paton Classic Wool, 100% wool,
3.5 oz (100 g)/223 yds (205 m)
Aran #202, 1 skein

Hooks
US H/8 (5 mm) and US I/9 (5.5 mm), *or sizes
you need to obtain correct gauge*

Gauge
14 sts and 12 rows = 4" × 4" (10 cm × 10 cm)
in hdc, with larger hook

Other supplies
Large-eye yarn needle

Abbreviations/Techniques
BPdc = back post double crochet (see
Some Special Techniques on page 98)
ch = chain
dc = double crochet
dec = decrease (see Some Special Techniques
on page 98)
FPdc = front post double crochet (see Some
Special Techniques on page 98)
hdc = half double crochet
sc = single crochet
yo = yarn over

SOME SPECIAL TECHNIQUES

This hat includes several techniques that you may not have run into before if you're a relatively new crocheter. Here's how to do them:

Back Post Double Crochet (BPdc): Yo hook, insert hook from back to front to back around indicated stitch, yo and draw up a loop; yo and draw through 2 loops, yo and draw through remaining 2 loops.

Back Post Double Crochet

Front Post Double Crochet (FPdc): Yo hook, insert hook from front to back to front around indicated stitch, yo and draw up a loop, yo and draw through 2 loops, yo and draw through remaining 2 loops.

Decrease (dec): (yo, pull up loop in next stitch) twice; yo and draw through all 5 loops on hook.

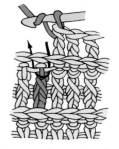

Front Post Double Crochet

CABLE PATTERN STITCH

(over 4 stitches; for FPdc and BPdc, see Some Special Techniques)

Row 1 Skip the first 2 stitches; FPdc in each of the next 2 stitches, FPdc in first skipped stitch, FPdc in second skipped stitch.

Row 2 BPdc in each of 4 FPdc stitches in the previous row. *Note:* Whenever you work either Front or Back Post dc, skip the stitches behind the FPdc or BPdc, and work the next stitch in the row as directed.

	CROCHETING THE RIBBING
NOTE	The ribbing is crocheted as a long strip, about 2" (5 cm) wide and 19" (47.5 cm) long. When it is completed, you will pick up the row stitches along the long edge to begin crocheting the cables that form the hat.
SET UP	With smaller hook, ch 10.
Row 1	Sc in second chain from hook and each chain to end; turn. *You now have 9 sc.*
Row 2	Ch 1, working in back loops only, sc in each stitch to end of row; turn.
Next Rows	Repeat Row 2 until piece measures approximately 19" (48.2 cm). Do not fasten off after last row.
	CROCHETING THE CABLES
SET UP	With larger hook, ch 2, 77 hdc evenly along one long edge of the Ribbing. Place a marker at beginning of this row to indicate Right Side; turn. Tip: Count the number of "ribs" you have and distribute your new stitches accordingly. Over each 3 "ribs," you will probably need to hdc about 7 sts.
Row 1 (wrong side)	Ch 2, hdc in each stitch to end of row; turn.
Row 2	Ch 2, hdc in next 2 hdc, * FPdc around next hdc, hdc in next 3 hdc, work Row 1 of Cable Pattern Stitch over next 4 stitches, hdc in next 3 hdc; repeat from * to end of row (the last repeat will have only 1 hdc after cable); turn.
Row 3	Ch 2, hdc in next 2 hdc, * work Row 2 of Cable Pattern Stitch over next 4 stitches, hdc in next 3 hdc, BPdc over next post stitch in previous row, hdc in next 3 hdc; repeat from * to end of row (the last repeat will have only 2 hdc after the single BPdc); turn.

Row 4	Ch 2, hdc in next 2 hdc, * FPdc over next post stitch in previous row, hdc in next 3 hdc, work Row 1 of Cable Pattern Stitch over next 4 post stitches in previous row, hdc in next 3 hdc; repeat from * to end of row (the last repeat will have 2 hdc after cable); turn.
Next Rows	Repeat Rows 3 and 4 five more times.
SHAPING THE TOP	
Row 1	Ch 2, hdc in next 2 hdc, * work Row 2 of Cable Pattern Stitch over next 4 stitches, hdc in next stitch, decrease over next 2 hdc (see Some Special Techniques), work BPdc over post stitch, hdc in next stitch, decrease over next 2 hdc; repeat from * to end of row; (the last repeat will have 21 hdc after cable) turn.
Row 2	Ch 2, hdc in next stitch, * FPdc over post stitch, decrease over next 2 hdc, work Row 1 of Cable Pattern Stitch over next 4 stitches, decrease over next 2 hdc; repeat from * to end of row (the last repeat will have 2 hdc after the cable); turn.
Row 3	Ch 2, hdc in next stitch, * pull up loop in top of next stitch and leave loop on hook, work Row 2 of Cable Pattern Stitch over next 4 stitches, finish stitch by drawing yo through all loops on hook; pull up loop in top of next stitch and leave loop on hook, work first BPdc over post stitch, finish stitch by drawing yo through all loops on hook, complete cable over next 3 stitches; repeat from * to end of row (last repeat will have only 1 hdc after the cable); turn.
Row 4	Ch 2, * hdc in next 2 stitches, decrease over next 2 stitches; repeat from * to end of row; turn.
Row 5	Ch 2, * hdc in next stitch, decrease over next 2 stitches; repeat from * to end of row; turn.
Row 6	Ch 2, (decrease over 2 stitches) to end of row.

FINISHING	
	Draw yarn through last stitch to fasten off, then, leaving a long tail for sewing the back seam, break yarn.
	Weave the long tail through the remaining stitches on the last row to draw it up, then use it to sew the back seam. When you get to the ribbing, reverse the seam so that when you turn up the cuff, the seam is on the inside. Turn up the cuff.

A TOUCH OF IRELAND

The creative stitch patterns we identify with Aran-style sweaters were originally knit with undyed homespun yarn. As practical and tough as they were beautiful, these sweaters were a product of a cottage industry begun on the islands off the west coast of Ireland in the early twentieth century. Several books adapting the knitted patterns to crochet designs have appeared in recent years, including two by Jane Snedden Peever.

Tweed & Bobbles

Bobbles and clusters make this hat a standout. Rugged yet soft tweed yarn in a variety of warm colors provides the perfect back drop for the fun texture. The combination of simple stitches complements this richly hued hat.

Finished measurement
22" (55.8 cm) circumference

Yarn
DK-weight wool tweed, 1 ball each of burnt orange, dark purple, and scarlet
I used Rowan Yorkshire Tweed DK, 100% wool, 125 yd/113 m, 1¾ oz/50 g balls
MC = Cheer 343, 1 ball
CA = Scarlet 344, 1 ball
CB = Revel 342, 1 ball

Hook
US G/6 (4.0 or 4.25 mm), *or size you need to obtain correct gauge*

Gauge
14 sts and 8 rows = 4" × 4" (10 cm × 10 cm) in dc

Other supplies
Large-eye yarn needle

Abbreviations and Special Terms
ch = chain
dc = double crochet
FPtr = Front Post triple crochet
hdc = half double crochet
sc = single crochet
tr cluster = triple cluster
yo = yarn over

CROCHETING THE HAT	
NOTE	At the end of each round, join with a slip stitch, but do not turn. The chains at the beginning of each round are used to create height for the stitches that follow; they do not count as stitches.
SET UP	Using MC, ch 4, join with a slip stitch in first ch to form a ring.
Round 1	Ch 1, 8 sc into ring, join to first sc. *You now have* 8 sc.
Round 2	Ch 2, 2 hdc in each sc around, join to first hdc. *You now have* 16 hdc.
Round 3	Ch 1, 2 sc in each hdc around, join to first sc. *You now have* 32 sc.
Round 4	* 2 dc in first stitch, dc in next 2 stitches; repeat from * 9 more times, dc in last 2 stitches. Fasten off MC, and change to CA, ch 1. *You now have* 42 dc.
Round 5	* Sc in the first 5 stitches, work tr cluster in round below; repeat from * to end of round. *Note:* The triple cluster counts as 1 stitch. At the end of this round you should have the same number of stitches (42) as you began with.
Round 6	Ch 2, hdc in each stitch to end of round (including tr clusters), join to beginning chain. *You now have* 42 hdc.
Round 7	Ch 3, dc in each stitch to end of round. In last stitch, fasten off CA , and change to MC.
Round 8	Ch 2, beginning with first stitch, * hdc in next 2 stitches, 2 hdc in next stitch; repeat from * to end of round, join to first hdc. *You now have* 56 hdc.
Round 9	Ch 1, * sc in next 2 stitches, tr cluster in row below, sc in next 3 stitches, 2 sc in next stitch; repeat from * to end of round, join to first sc.
Round 10	Ch 2, * hdc in each stitch to end of round (including tr clusters), join to first hdc. *You now have* 56 hdc.

Round 11	Ch 3, * dc in next 7 stitches, 2 dc in next stitch; repeat from * to end of round. In last stitch, fasten off MC, and change to CA. Join to first dc. *You now have* 63 dc.
Round 12	Ch 1, * sc in the first 4 stitches, work 2 sc in next stitch, sc in next 3 stitches, tr cluster in row below; repeat from * to end of round, join to first sc.
Round 13	Ch 2, hdc in each stitch around (including tr cluster), join to first hdc. *You now have* 70 hdc.
Round 14	Ch 3, * dc in next 34 stitches, work 2 dc in the next stitch; repeat from * once. In last stitch, fasten off CA, and change to CB. Join to first dc. *You now have* 72 dc.
Round 15	Ch 1, beginning in first stitch, * sc in next 3 stitches, dc in row below; repeat from * to end of round, join to first sc. *You now have* 18 dc. *Note:* The "dc in the row below" counts as 1 stitch; do not dc in the corresponding stitch in the active round.

TRIPLE CLUSTER

This hat is ornamented with bobbles created with a triple cluster (tr cluster) stitch. In the row beneath the active row, work 3 FPtr around the stitch directly below the next stitch in the active row as follows:

    * yo twice, insert hook from front to back to front around stitch, yo, pull through a loop, (yo and draw through 2 loops) twice (you now have 2 loops on hook); repeat from * 2 more times (you now have 4 loops on hook), yo and draw through all loops on hook.

Round 16	Ch 3, dc in each stitch around, join to first dc. Fasten off CB, and change to CA.
Round 17	Ch 1, sc in first stitch, * dc in row below, sc in next 3 stitches; repeat from * to last 2 stitches, 2 sc, join to first sc.
Round 18	Ch 3, dc in each stitch to end of round, join to first dc.
Round 19	Ch 3, * dc in next 13 stitches, work 2 dc in next stitch; repeat from * to last 2 stitches, 2 sc. In last stitch, fasten off CA, and change to CB. Join to first dc. *You now have* 77 dc.
Round 20	Ch 1, beginning in first stitch, * sc in next 6 stitches, tr cluster in row below; repeat from * to end of round, join to first sc.
Round 21	Ch 3, dc in each stitch to end of round, join to first dc. *You now have* 77 dc.
Round 22	Ch 3, beginning in first stitch, * dc in next 9 stitches, work 2 dc together; repeat from * to end of round, join to first dc. *You now have* 70 dc.
Round 22	Ch 2, skip first stitch, * hdc in next 2 stitches, (hdc, ch 4, slip stitch to fourth chain from top) in next stitch; repeat from * to end of round, join to first hdc.

FINISHING

	Draw yarn through last stitch to fasten off, then break yarn. Weave any loose ends into the wrong side of the hat.

Acknowledgments

I want to thank the many people who work so tirelessly behind the scenes.
Without them this book wouldn't have been possible:

First of all, I couldn't do any of this without the support and dedication of Joyce Nordstrom.
She is the one person who pulls all my designs together, and along with her helpers,
Judy Timmer and Jane Lind, she makes my work so much easier.

Thanks to all the people behind the scenes at Storey,
including Cindy McFarland, art director, and Jen Smith, production designer,
and especially to Gwen Steege, my editor, who is always kind and patient
even when I'm behind schedule.

Finally I want to thank my family, Tom, Jonathan, Heather, John, Johnny, Rajeana,
and Melody, because with them I'm more complete.

Sources

Berroco, Inc.
P.O. Box 367
14 Elmdale Road
Uxbridge, MA 01569-0367
www.berroco.com

Cascade
www.cascadeyarns.com

Classic Elite Yarns
122 Western Ave.
Lowell, MA 01851-1434
www.classiceliteyarns.com

Coats & Clark
Consumer Services
P.O. Box 12229
Greenville, SC 29612-0229
www.coatsandclark.com

Judi & Co
631-499-8480
www.judiandco.com
judico@optonline.net

Lion Brand Yarn
135 Kero Road
Carlstadt, NJ 07072
www.lionbrand.com

Nashua
4 Townsend West, Unit 8
Nashua, NH 03063

Patons
P.O. Box 40
320 Livingstone Avenue South
Listowel, Ontario N4W 3H3
Canada
www.patonsyarns.com

Rowan Yarns
4 Townsend West, Unit 8
Nashua, NH 03063
www.knitrowan.com

Wendy: See Berroco

Index

Page numbers for charts are in **bold**; those for photos and illustrations are in *italics*.

Abbreviations and symbols, 11, **11**
American (U.S.) hook sizes, **18**
Angora & Diamonds, 72–75, *73,* **74–75**
Aran-Style Cables, 96–101, *97–98,* **99–101**
asterisk symbol, 11

Baby, Sherbet-Topped, 42–45, *43,* **44–45,** *45*
back loop (bl), 10, **11**
back post double crochet (BPdc), 98, *98*
Beaded (Pearl) Cap, 13, 52–55, *53,* **54–55,** *55*
beads, working with, 13–14, *13–14,* 54
Bobbles & Tweed, 102–6, *103,* **104–6,** *105*
brackets symbol, 11
British terms. *See* U.K. (English)

Cables, Aran-Style, 96–101, *97–98,* **99–101**
care instructions, 25
chain (ch), **11,** 19–20, *19–20*
Chain (Gold) juliet, 82–85, *83,* **84–85**
Child, Flower, 90–95, *91,* **92–94,** *94–95*
circles, working with, 28–29, *28–29*
Cloche, Dressy, 86–89, *87,* **88–89,** 89
Colorful Sun Hat, 62–67, *63,* **64–67,** *67*
Continental (metric) hook sizes, **18**
crochet bag, contents of, 16, *16*
crocheting, 6–30
    abbreviations and symbols, 11, **11**
    beads, working with, 13–14, *13–14,* 54
    care instructions, 25
    circles, working with, 28–29, *28–29*
    fiber content of yarn, 8, 9, 25
    finishes, 15–16, *15–16*
    finishing projects, 30, *30*
    gauge (swatch), 12, *12,* 25

holding the hook and yarn, 17–18, *17–18*
hooks, 7, *7,* 12, 16, *16–17,* 17, **18,** 25
joining yarn, 29, *29*
knots, avoiding, 29
sources for, 109
wearability and yarn choice, 8
weight and ply of yarns, 9, **9,** 25
yarns, 8–9, *8–9,* 12, 18, *18,* 25

Dagger symbol, 11
decrease (dec), **11,** 59, 98
Diamonds & Angora, 72–75, *73,* **74–75**
double crochet (dc), **11,** 17, 22–23, *22–23,* **24**
double treble (dtr), **24**
Dressy Cloche, 86–89, *87,* **88–89,** 89
dye lots of yarn, 9

Edgings, beaded, 14
English terms. *See* U.K. (English)

Fair Isle Hat, 68–71, *69,* **70–71**
Faux-Suede Helmet, 56–61, *57,* **58–61,** *59, 61*
fiber content of yarn, 8, 9, 25
finishes, 15–16, *15–16*
finishing projects, 30, *30*
Flower Child, 90–95, *91,* **92–94,** *94–95*
flowers, beaded, *13,* 13–14
Flowers, Retro, 76–81, *77,* **78–80,** *81*
four-strand braid, making a, 50, *50*
front loop (fl), 10, **11**
front post double crochet (FPdc), 98, *98*

Gauge (swatch), 12, *12,* 25
Gold-Chain Juliet, 82–85, *83,* **84–85**